AMERICAN POLITICS
AND
CATHOLIC CHRISTIANITY

ISSUES OF CONSCIENCE
& DEFINED MORAL DOCTRINE

AMERICAN POLITICS AND CATHOLIC CHRISTIANITY

ISSUES OF CONSCIENCE & DEFINED MORAL DOCTRINE

—— * ——

GERALD GOODRUM

SECOND EDITION

ISBN 978-1–4811189-6-5

Religion . . . is not a problem for legislators to solve, but a vital contributor to the national conversation. In this light, I cannot but voice my concern at the increasing marginalization of religion, particularly of Christianity, that is taking place in some quarters, even in nations which place a great emphasis on tolerance. There are those who would advocate that the voice of religion be silenced, or at least relegated to the purely private sphere. There are those who argue that the public celebration of festivals such as Christmas should be discouraged, in the questionable belief that it might somehow offend those of other religions or none. And there are those who argue—paradoxically with the intention of eliminating discrimination—that Christians in public roles should be required at times to act against their conscience. These are worrying signs of a failure to appreciate not only the rights of believers to freedom of conscience and freedom of religion, but also the legitimate role of religion in the public square.

—POPE BENEDICT XVI

Benedict XVI, "Address to the British Parliament" (17 September 2010). Available from http://www.vatican.va/holy_father/benedict_xvi/speeches/2010/september/documents/hf_ben-xvi_spe_20100917_societa-civile_en.html; Internet; accessed 22 January 2012.

Contents

Introduction

According to a recently published study on religions, there are more people who profess Christianity in the United States of America than in any other nation on earth.[1] Among these Christians, the most numerous body is the Catholic Church. In fact, surveys show that in the United States the number of Catholics dwarfs that of all other singular Christian affiliations along with all other religious non-Christian organizations.[2] In theory, one could be led to assume that the reality behind these statistical facts would translate into an influence of the Catholic Church's teachings on morality in the practical matters of the American political landscape. After all, the United States of America is not only a constitutional republic but a representative democracy, and if its government is "of the people, by the people, [and] for the people,"[3] and if a great number of these "people" are now Catholic, then the conclusion seems obvious. Unfortunately, when this syllogism meets reality, it somehow implodes, and therein lies the rub. On the other hand, what would it be like if circumstances were different than they currently are? It is to that end that this book attempts to make a modest contribution.

The contents of this book, then, given the sheer number of Christians in general and Catholic Christians in particular, merely serve to back up a single claim: the person who would aspire to public office in the United States of America who does not respect Christians or the fundamental tenets of Christianity should not receive the Catholic Christian vote. That statement does not preclude voting for those who are non-Christian, and it certainly does not mean that Catholics should automatically vote for fellow Catholics.

There exist non-Christians who are respectful of Jesus and who on many levels are in accord with the teachings of the Catholic Church regarding morality, the nature of marriage and family life. The United States might not be a Christian nation *per se*; however, given the historical importance of Christianity which informed the construction of the Declaration of Independence, the Articles of Confederation and the Constitution, the additional facts that the early European colonizers were Christians and that to this day Christians are overwhelmingly the majority, one thing is clear: religious faith is a decisive issue when it comes to the way in which people of the United States organize themselves in community according to laws and regulations that strive to be just—otherwise known as politics.

*

It is to be mentioned from the outset what this book is not. This book is not an attempt to promote or demote any one political party or candidate. To do so would be to assume that political parties are monolithic in their platforms and ideas, that every candidate equally represents his or her party, and that one particular party possibly achieves the ideals a Catholic voter is looking for when he or she votes. As one examines the political spectrum, one finds on deeper research that the political parties are far from being monolithic, that there is great variation among representatives and that many (if not most) elected officials and candidates fall far beneath being *ideal* to the Catholic voter.

*

On a philosophic level, undergirding this book is an appeal to philosophical realism and the principles of logic in an attempt to expose and to confront immoral and potentially nihilistic practices currently holding sway in specific American policies. As a method, it could be said that I employ phenomenology in not only penetrating and opening up issues, but also by describing them in their different aspects. Stylistically, the text varies from formal to informal language depending upon whether an issue is treated in its fundamental nature (technical and philosophical: *transcendentalese*) or as the issue is commonly regarded or typically seen in everyday society and culture (nontechnical and conversational: *mundanese*).[4]

Along with philosophical and theological arguments, I also appeal to emotions, sensibilities and public perceptions in the discussion of these themes. Many people form opinions and make decisions based on their heart and not their head (the rational faculty) and the appeal of rhetoric is as much to sentiments as it is to hard logic. In this regard, the text could be said to be controversial or even polemical but I maintain that Christianity is such at its core. *Jesus of Nazareth, the Christ, is controversial. Catholicism, which offers a "Christocentric" and "Theologic" vision of the world, is controversial.*

As an example of this polemic: in the chapter regarding the conscience, some people may disapprove of my assessment of the then Senator John F. Kennedy and his 1960 Houston "Speech on Faith"; however, I state up front that I am of a generation of Catholics which has neither admiration for nor an emotive attachment to the thirty-fifth President of the United States. In this work I do attempt to be charitable, but I believe in a Catholicism which is equally as offensive as it is defensive. In that way, I actually highlight several cultural idols, such as Kennedy and Lady Gaga, and critique aspects of their forms of argumentation and influential cultural sway.

*

This work is meant for the Catholic voter and for the most part preaches to the choir. Although the choir might be able to sing, it is not infrequent to find members of the choir who are unable to articulate why the choir is singing what it is singing. This book reflects the desire to explain *why* the Catholic Church teaches *what* she teaches about certain politically relevant fundamental issues of faith and morals. In doing so, it is important to mention that the teachings of the Catholic Church are not in opposition to reason but are rather supported by it: hence, faith *and* reason (*fides* et *ratio*)—not faith *or* reason (*fides* aut *ratio*). The Catholic Faith carries within itself an inner logic which becomes explicit as one's personal act of faith is manifested in words and deeds. This understanding is given in 1 Peter 3:15, where it is written: "Be ready everywhere and at all times to give reason to the hope that is within you."

While there are many issues at play with regards to the Christian voter, this text limits itself to the exploration of merely several: (1) what is meant by freedom of religion; (2) the conscience and President John F. Kennedy's false dichotomies; (3) being pro-life vs. pro-abortion; (4) a fundamental analysis of marriage regarded properly between one man and one woman; and (5) the same-sex agenda as a societal tsunami. Admittedly, other themes—such as those of social justice, the environment, immigration, economic policies and the medical care system in general—could have been included in this present volume. They are not here for at least three reasons: (1) given my other commitments, I did not have the time to write about them; (2) the United States Conference of Catholic Bishops (USCCB) has issued a document entitled *Forming Consciences for Faithful Citizenship: A Call to Political Responsibility from the Catholic Bishops of the United States*,[5] which treats such topics rather substantively; (3) the Catholic Church's position on the issues discussed in *this* book is considered settled, is of a definitive and perennial nature, and therefore of interest to me as a student of philosophy and theology. On the other hand, there are various approaches at the level of "prudential judgment" regarding the demands of social justice, the environment, immigration, economic policies, and the medical care system; and it is my opinion that elected public officials (whether Democrat, Republican, or Independent) are most qualified to accomplish these shared goals according to what they determine is best, provided that the dignity of the human person is given paramount consideration.

*

For me this book is a project, an experiment, and a first edition. There was much fun in writing it and my hope is that it will at least provide an impetus for a deeper conversation on politics, Catholicism, and issues of conscience and morality. Lastly, it should be stated that the analyses presented in this book make no claim to be either academic or comprehensive.

CHAPTER I

Religious Freedom

The Commonplace Persecution of Christians

The teachings of Jesus have always been taken as polemical and controversial to pagan, materialist and secularist societies. Jesus was publicly humiliated and put to death for what He said and taught. The first Pope (Peter), the other Apostles (save John the Evangelist, who was persecuted and forced into exile before he died), Paul of Tarsus, and numerous other early followers of Jesus were publicly martyred for promoting Christianity. Catholics throughout the centuries who evangelized Europe were put to death by emperors and the pagan tribes which they encountered. During the evangelization of the New World, thousands upon thousands of Catholics lost their lives in spreading the Christian Faith. Let us not forget that even as recently as the 1920s and 1930s and as close to home as "Catholic" Mexico many people were martyred for the Faith by anti-Catholic regimes. Also, under National Socialism and Communism in the twentieth century the Church suffered and many Catholics died in concentration camps and prisons, and by torture or direct execution. Currently around the globe, especially in the Arabic, Asiatic and African nations, it is dangerous to be a Christian, and martyrs are being made every day for profession of faith in Jesus of Nazareth. Christianity is the most persecuted religion in the world and many Christians presently live in fear for their life.[6] This is merely a cursory overview of the plight of the Church persecuted throughout the world, but nevertheless a poignant reminder of what is at stake in following the Christ.

With all of the persecution of the Church in the world, why should we here in the United States not suffer or even be ready to die on account of the Gospel? The Constitution and its Amendments, and the form of government of the United States itself, for the most part reflect the teachings of Christianity. In fact, until the latter part of the twentieth century, the policies and laws for citizens of the United States were largely compatible with Catholicism since they affirmed and upheld basic human rights stemming from the natural law.[7] Toward the end of the last century, however, things began to change and at the beginning of the third millennium circumstances have progressed dramatically in hostility toward Catholicism and the teachings of Jesus of Nazareth.

The First Amendment[8]

Of course, the Church in the United States is no stranger to persecution as a significant number of Catholic immigrants in the nineteenth and the first half of the twentieth centuries were ostracized, denied work and were victims of hate crimes. However, this new ostracization and persecution is not the result of Protestant anti-Catholic rhetoric (for many Protestants who adhere to biblical teaching and values are now in the same boat as the Catholic Church), but is rather the result of a type of godlessness and secularity which the United States has not witnessed since its founding. For instance, there is a growing number of people in political office who interpret the First Amendment to mean that the United States should be free from religion.[9] According to this interpretation, religion is to exist only in the private sphere (on Friday [Islam], on Saturday [Judaism], on Sunday [Christianity]) and is not to have an impact in any way on one's public life and responsibilities. Freedom of "worship" is granted but not freedom of religion. The God of Abraham is not to be mentioned and certainly not to be invoked in public, so as not to "offend anyone." The understanding is that politics is a-religious and that politicians are therefore not to be associated with religious faith. A further disturbing by-product of this assumption is that when issues which are moral in nature overlap with politics, these are best decided by those "authorities" in public office as elected or appointed officials without any reference to religion. In this way, politics (the realm of the State) replaces religion (the realm of the Church) and begins to pronounce on the ultimate meaning of life and, of course, without any reference to a Being more transcendent than itself.

This interpretation of the First Amendment is misguided and false. The Amendment states: "Congress shall make no law respecting an establishment of religion, or prohibiting the free exercise thereof; or abridging the freedom of speech, or of the press; or the right of the people peaceably to assemble, and to petition the Government for a redress of grievances."[10] It is well documented that the original thirteen colonies of the United States were settled by a group of people who were seeking a place to be free in order to adhere to the tenets, practice and expression of their religion.[11] Given that they were attacked and persecuted in England for their faith, they were willing to make a perilous journey and face unparalleled sacrifices and found a new land where they would be free precisely to live according to their faith without having the interference of an authoritarian government. Thus, the correct interpretation of what are known as the Establishment and Free Exercise Clauses of the First Amendment is and must be freedom *for* religion.

In what could be taken as a commentary on these two clauses of the First Amendment, Pope Benedict XVI writes:

[17]

The just ordering of society and the State is a central responsibility of politics. As Augustine once said, a State which is not governed according to justice would be just a bunch of thieves: *Remota itaque iustitia quid sunt regna nisi magna latrocinia?*[12] Fundamental to Christianity is the distinction between what belongs to Caesar and what belongs to God,[13] in other words, the distinction between Church and State, or, as the Second Vatican Council puts it, the autonomy of the temporal sphere.[14] The State may not impose religion, yet it must guarantee religious freedom and harmony between the followers of different religions. For her part, the Church, as the social expression of Christian faith, has a proper independence and is structured on the basis of her faith as a community which the State must recognize. The two spheres are distinct, yet always interrelated.[15]

This helps one understand that the first words of the First Amendment were placed there to protect religion and conscience from the intrusions of government and to set up a proper "interrelated" autonomy (as explained by the Holy Father), not an absolute and inimical one to the tyrannical exclusion of the other. Furthermore, it should be noted that for the first words of the First Amendment to concern religious faith emphasizes the importance of religion and its protection and freedom of expression to the Founders of the United States.

Attacks on Religious Freedom

How is the Church presently being persecuted in the United States? For an answer, I turn to Timothy Cardinal Dolan. On October 20, 2011, the Archbishop of New York and President of the United States Conference of Catholic Bishops (USCCB) penned an article on religious freedom for a column in his archdiocesan newspaper, articulating the following eight points:

1. For five acclaimed years, the Migration and Refugee Services of the Catholic bishops has received a government grant assisting close to 3,000 victims of human trafficking rebuild their lives after escaping bondage, to obtain food, clothing, safety and health care. All agreed the Church provided this service lovingly and effectively. [16] No more. Just last month, the government funds were denied. While no convincing reason has yet to be given, the chilling warning seems clear: If you don't offer "reproductive services"—abortion, contraception, sterilization—you will no longer get grants from Health and Human Services. Government regulation would now require a faith-based group to violate its conscience.

2. The intrusion does not stop here. The same Health and Human Services has mandated that most Catholic employers, including hospitals, charities and universities, add the same such "services" in their health plans.

3. The threat to religious freedom goes on: Catholic Relief Services, the renowned international agency bringing medicine, food, shelter and education to the hungry and stricken of the world, is learning that its ability to partner with the foreign aid programs of our government is being compromised because they refuse to violate their consciences in providing such "services." [17]

4. In Alabama, the state lectured the churches and synagogues that they were not to serve "illegals" in

their charitable and educational outreach. When people of faith pleaded that such a restriction violated the basic principles of their conscience, and brought their concerns to court, they lost.

5. In at least two states and our nation's capital, Catholic agencies long heralded for providing the most professional adoption services, are closing up, since the state is coercing them to place children with same-sex couples, something people of faith respond they are unable to do.

6. And just last week, the government argued before the Supreme Court for the effective gutting of the longstanding "ministerial exception" that allows religious bodies to hire and fire ministerial employees without government interference. This extreme position has drawn criticism from nearly every major religious organization in the country, from liberal to conservative, from the National Council of Churches to the National Association of Evangelicals, all of whom fear that their churches could be the next targets of an intrusive Uncle Sam.[18]

7. We bishops—and a growing number of pastors and leaders of other creeds—are very worried. That the right to the free exercise of religion is listed as the first in our Bill of Rights is itself eloquent testimony to its pivotal place in the foundation of our Republic.

8. Today, though, Freedom of Religion is being reduced to a "freedom of worship," a personal hobby on one's Sabbath, tolerated as long as the values expressed in that hour of worship have no impact at all in society. Such a view is, of course, contrary to religion itself, which hardly looks at faith as anything but a normative influence on one's life, having a defining sway in how one dreams, plans, works, serves, and even votes.[19]

This litany of attacks on religious freedom and on the services provided by the Church should disturb every Catholic and should awaken us to become more conscientious in the way we view those in public office. Not only should the bishops be "very worried," but also every Catholic and other persons of good will. Likewise, in the same article, the Cardinal describes our current situation as "a genuine crisis, as certain well-placed, well-financed people, with a misplaced zeal they usually attribute to the religious people they enjoy caricaturing, seem set on a roll-back of the freedom of religion at the heart of this country." [20]

Catholics in the United States can no longer afford to play games or to stand idly by while the Church's teachings and practices come under threat from a government whose Bill of Rights expressly prohibits coercive measures which deny religious freedom. [21] The First Amendment to the Constitution protects the Catholic Church and all Christian and non-Christian religious affiliations from being trampled on by those in office. We must ensure that this remains the case.

However, increasingly in recent years, there has been a *de facto* encroachment of governmental policies into the domain and territory of the Catholic Church regarding issues of conscience and morality. But it must be emphatically stated that no person or government has any right or authority to dictate to the Catholic Church what she is to believe or teach. The Church and institutions affiliated with or operated by her should have the freedom to exist in accordance with Christian teachings. Universities, schools, hospitals, clinics, insurances, orphanages, charities and every other type of entity established and maintained by the Catholic Church should have the freedom to express and to adhere to Christian moral principles. Otherwise, this list of grievances noted by a commentator at *CatholicCulture.org* will only continue to grow. He observes:

Unfortunately, with each passing year our society shows less and less tolerance for the individual conscience. An overweening government requires Christians to accept the prevailing moral norms even when they violate the principles of Christian morality, and powerful private institutions only add to the pressure.

Consider the restrictions that a Catholic—and especially a young Catholic—now faces on the job market (I write from the perspective of a Catholic. But the same problems apply, with more or less equal force, to others who share the Catholic perspective on these moral issues).

A Catholic who cannot in good conscience sign the marriage certificate of two homosexual lovers may be unable to serve as town clerk in states that recognize same-sex "marriage."

A Catholic pharmacist who refuses to dispense abortifacient pills may not be allowed to continue his practice, where law requires him to provide customers with the "morning-after" pill (not to mention ordinary contraceptive pills, which have abortifacient properties).

A Catholic innkeeper who declines to play host to the celebration of homosexual unions may be stripped of his license to take paying guests [or an even more common consideration, consider a Catholic who would refuse to rent to couples of the same sex].

A Catholic medical student who objects to involvement in abortion or sterilization may find that only a few hospitals will consider him as an applicant for residency or internship.

A Catholic social worker who recognizes the injustice of placing foster children in homosexual households will be unable to find work in a state-funded adoption agency.

A Catholic police officer can lose his job if he hesitates to arrest someone seeking to dissuade a young woman from entering an abortion clinic.

A Catholic psychiatrist who clings to the age-old understanding that homosexuality is a disorder may be blackballed by his colleagues, ridiculed by the media, and possibly deprived of his professional accreditation.

And now a Catholic clerk who objects to cutting checks for birth-control pills will be unable to work at any American health-insurance company.

All of the above might be classified as forms of job discrimination: Catholics Need Not Apply. But the pressure is mounting, and Catholics are being discouraged from entry into more and more jobs—especially in the fields where the Church has been most active, the fields of health, education, and welfare. It is vitally important for American Catholics to recognize the trend and reverse it, before the word "discrimination" is too mild to describe the government's hostility.[22]

Catholics are everywhere, not just within Church structures, and governmental policies which coerce and obligate us to go against Christian principles are unjust and should not be tolerated. Pope John Paul II, in an address to members of the European Parliament, poignantly sums up the current predicament:

The competence of the State . . . is only to administer the external aspects of the earthly city. It may not claim to teach the ultimate meaning of human existence, or to bring about final happiness, or to override the human conscience. It is not entitled to enforce atheism or to discriminate against citizens on the ground of their religion. The Church always retains the right to proclaim the Gospel, to administer the sacraments, and to exercise pastoral care over its members.[23]

This only serves to heighten the importance of the role of Catholics in the public square. As discrimination increases, so should the volume of our voices.

The HHS Mandate: Violations of Conscience and Religious Freedom

On January 20, 2012, the USCCB issued a letter in question-and-answer format entitled, "The HHS Mandate for Contraception/Sterilization Coverage: An Attack on Rights of Conscience." Here, given the letter's well-written, thorough and comprehensive style, I reproduce it in full:

> *How important is the right of conscience in American tradition?*
> It has always been of paramount importance: "No provision in our Constitution ought to be dearer to man than that which protects the rights of conscience against the enterprises of the civil authority" (Thomas Jefferson, 1809).
> *In the past, has the federal government respected conscientious objections to procedures such as sterilization that may violate religious beliefs or moral convictions?*
> Yes. For example, a law in effect since 1973 says that no individual is required to take part in "any part of a health service program or research activity funded in whole or in part under a program administered by the Secretary of Health and Human Services" if it is "contrary to his religious beliefs or moral convictions" (42 USC 300a-7 [d]). Even the Federal Employees Health Benefits Program, which requires most of its health plans to cover

contraception, exempts religiously affiliated plans and protects the conscience rights of health professionals in the other plans. Currently no federal law requires anyone to purchase, sell, sponsor, or be covered by a private health plan that violates his conscience.

How has the Department of Health and Human Services departed from this policy?

By issuing a mandate for coverage of sterilization and contraceptives (including long-lasting injections and implants, and "morning-after" pills that may cause an early abortion) in virtually all private health plans. In August 2011 HHS included these procedures in a list of 'preventive services for women' to be required in health plans issued on or after August 1, 2012. On January 20, 2012, HHS reaffirmed its mandate while deferring enforcement against some religious employers until August 2013.

Is it appropriate to require coverage of these as "preventive services"?

No. The other services on HHS's list seek to prevent serious disease—breast cancer, lung cancer, AIDS. Pregnancy is not a disease. The Institute of Medicine committee that compiled the "preventive services" list for HHS said in its report that unintended pregnancy is "a condition for which safe and effective prevention and treatment" needs to be more widely available—setting the stage for mandated coverage of abortion as the "treatment" when prevention fails. Note that women who suffer from infertility, which really is an illness, were ignored in this mandate.

Didn't HHS include a religious exemption?

Yes, an incredibly narrow "religious employer" exemption that fails to protect many, perhaps most, religious employers. To be eligible an organization must meet four strict criteria, including the requirement that it both hire and serve primarily people of its own faith. Catholic schools and hospitals would have to eject their non-Catholic employees, students and patients, or purchase health coverage that violates their moral and religious teaching. Jesus and his apostles would not have been "religious enough" for the exemption, since they healed and served people of different faiths. The exemption provides no protection at all to sponsors and providers of health plans for the general public, to pro-life people who own businesses, or to individuals with a moral or religious objection to these procedures.

Isn't this an aspect of the Administration's drive for broader access to health care for all?

Whether or not it was intended that way, it has the opposite effect. People will not be free to keep the coverage they have now that respects their convictions. Organizations with many employees will have to violate their consciences or stop offering health benefits altogether. And resources needed to provide basic health care to the uninsured will be used instead to facilitate IUDs and Depo-Provera for those who already had ample coverage. This is a diversion away from universal health care.

But won't this provide "free birth control" for American women?

That claim is false for two reasons. First, the coverage will be mandatory, not a matter of free choice for any woman. Second, insurance companies will not be able to charge a co-pay or deductible for the coverage, so they will simply add the cost to the standard premium everyone has to pay—and among those being required to pay will be people who oppose it on conscience grounds. That is no victory for freedom.

By objecting to this coverage, is the Catholic Church discriminating against women?

Not at all. The Church's teaching against early abortion is based on respect for all human life, male and female. Its teaching against contraception and sterilization is based on respect for the power to help generate a new human life, a power held by both men and women—so health plans in accord with Catholic teaching do not cover male or female sterilization. It is the HHS mandate that shows disregard for women, by forcing them to purchase this coverage whether they want it or not.

Do religious employers violate the consciences of women who want birth control, by refusing to cover it in their employee health plans?

No, they simply decline to provide active support for procedures that violate their own consciences. If an employee disagrees, he can simply purchase that coverage or those procedures elsewhere.

What solution to this dispute would be acceptable?

Ideally, HHS can leave the law the way it has always been, so those who provide, sponsor and purchase health coverage can make their own decisions about whether to include these procedures without the federal government imposing one answer on everyone. If HHS refuses, it will be especially urgent for Congress to pass the "Respect for Rights of Conscience Act" (HR 1179/S. 1467), to prevent [the] health care reform act from being used to violate insurers' and purchasers' moral and religious beliefs.[24]

This letter adequately rebuts the United States Department of Health and Human Services' mandate.[25] Still other considerations from a Catholic worldview regarding the mandate can be summarily stated as follows: (1) In general, no tax-payer money at any level should go to support contraception, abortifacients (chemical drugs that cause an early abortion), or sterilizations; for the State to coerce the Church to pay for such things, is tyrannical; (2) The State is dogmatizing on matters of morality by imposing an immorality on its citizens, violating the policy of separation of Church and State, impinging upon the freedom of religious institutions, and disregarding the consciences of people of faith; in essence, the State is being dictatorial; (3) Furthermore, when the sexual act through contraception or abortifacients is no longer open to life, then sexual promiscuity, the degradation of women into mere sex objects, and the aberration of nature known as sodomy are promoted; of course, logically same-sex "marriage" is condoned as being just one more form of intimate sexual expression that should be legal (these issues will be dealt with in the following chapters)—all of which firmly establish a State-induced hegemonic hedonism.[26]

Moreover, to place pregnancy in the category of diseases, health risks and "preventive services," as the HHS mandate does, is to equate the unborn human person with diseases, health risks and some *thing* to be prevented. In this context, it is important to keep in mind the words of Cardinal DiNardo of Galveston-Houston:

> Preventive services are aimed at preventing diseases (e.g., by vaccinations) or detecting them early to aid prompt treatment (e.g., screening for diabetes or cancer). But pregnancy is not a disease. It is the normal, healthy state by which each of us came into the world. Far from preventing disease, contraceptives can have serious health consequences of their own, for example, increasing the risk of acquiring a sexually transmitted disease, such as AIDS, increasing the risk of breast

cancer from excess estrogen, and of blood clots that can lead to stroke from synthetic progestin.[27] Mandating such coverage shows neither respect for women's health or freedom, nor respect for the consciences of those who do not want to take part in such problematic initiatives.[28]

Looking at the human person as the Department of Health and Human Services does is pessimistic, reductionist, utilitarian, and a far cry from the biblical view of the human person as "made in the image and likeness of God"[29] and the "inherent and transcendent dignity"[30] description given by the *Catechism of the Catholic Church*. However, that is precisely the way in which the HHS mandate categorizes human life. The HHS mandate, instead of adhering to the Gospel of Life, imposes a non-biblical gospel of prosperity: abort or use contraception, and be prosperous. This is not the Gospel of Life of the Bible which considers the ability to have (numerous) children a sign of divine blessing and favor.[31]

Finally, it is important here to note briefly that the dangerous agenda behind such a mandate has been germinating for decades and was lucidly exposed and warned against over forty years ago by Pope Paul VI in his Encyclical *Humanae Vitae*. After spelling out the consequences of methods and plans of artificial birth control as paving the way for widespread infidelity, the lowering of moral standards, the promoting of vice and in fact a temptation for the already natural human weakness in keeping the moral law, and the reduction of the woman to an instrument or object of satisfaction, Pope Paul VI states:

Careful consideration should be given to the danger of this power [of controlling births] passing into the hands of those public authorities who care little for the precepts of the moral law. Who will blame a government which in its attempt to resolve the problems affecting an entire country resorts to the same measures as are regarded as lawful by married people in the solution of a particular family difficulty? Who will prevent public authorities from favoring those contraceptive methods which they consider more effective? Should they regard this as necessary, they may even impose their use on everyone. It could well happen, therefore, that when people, either individually or in family or social life, experience the inherent difficulties of the divine law and are determined to avoid them, they may give into the hands of public authorities the power to intervene in the most personal and intimate responsibility of husband and wife.

Consequently, unless we are willing that the responsibility of procreating life should be left to the arbitrary decision of men, we must accept that there are certain limits, beyond which it is wrong to go, to the power of man over his own body and its natural functions—limits, let it be said, which no one, whether as a private individual or as a public authority, can lawfully exceed. These limits are expressly imposed because of the reverence due to the whole human organism and its natural functions.[32]

Philosophically, the Holy Father highlights the important respect that we are to have toward nature and our bodies in that there are natural limits to human action. Moreover, theologically, he reminds us that our bodies are temples of the Holy Spirit claimed by God to His honor and glory and not only our own. It is clear, then, that even as early as 1968, the Church was offering a clarion call against the infringement of the State upon the freedoms of her members when it concerns contraception, abortifacients and sterilizations. The fact that these types of mandates have been happening for years in countries like China and India provides for us in the "land of the free" at the beginning of the third millennium a further implication of such totalitarian practices which threaten not only human freedom and conscience but morality and humanity in general.

The Problematic HHS Mandate "Compromise"

On February 10, 2012, after a national outcry from Catholics, other religious communities and from men and women of the ranks of both Democrats and Republicans, a "compromise" regarding the HHS mandate was announced by the White House.[33] Unfortunately, the proposed solution did nothing but play a game of semantics as a group of university scholars notes:

> This so-called "accommodation" changes nothing of moral substance and fails to remove the assault on religious liberty and the rights of conscience which gave rise to the controversy. It is certainly no compromise. The reason for the original bipartisan uproar was the administration's insistence that religious employers, be they institutions or individuals, provide insurance that covered services they regard as gravely immoral and unjust. Under the new rule, the government still coerces religious institutions and individuals to purchase insurance policies that include the very same services.[34]

Simply put, the HHS mandate pre-compromise and post-compromise is substantially unchanged: (1) the religious institution pays for the insurance; (2) the insurance "freely" covers contraceptives, abortion-inducing drugs and steriliza- tions. The principle is, consequently, still the same and the logic is that of a vicious circle. The difference is that with the "compromise," the insurance companies are coerced directly to provide such services and not religious institutions (al- though the religious institutions are still paying for the in- surance). Thus, contrary to the First Amendment, the gov- ernment seeks to prohibit the free exercise of religion.

Moreover, relevant here is the following question: What about religious institutions which are self-insured[35] or what about the liberty of the non-religious private company that self-insures and that is unable now to refuse such so-called "preventive services"? This revised mandate, then, permits the government to dictate to a private company not only that it must offer a product, but the specific type of product to offer. With this "compromise," not only is the govern- ment violating the religious freedom guaranteed by the First Amendment, but now there is the added intrusion into other personal and private liberties.

Lastly, even if the HHS mandate should be considered null and void, it is nevertheless important to keep in mind its problematic nature and antireligious bias. A hermeneutic of suspicion is forever warranted toward those who would impose such a policy in the first place. As the saying goes: Once bitten, twice shy. Once the principle of freedom is breached, the limits to its violation are weakened, and how is one to know when further attacks are on their way?

CHAPTER II

The Conscience

I. THE CONSCIENCE AND RELATED ISSUES

Church Authority and Teaching

Given that the living authority of the teaching office of the Church (the Magisterium: the Pope and the bishops in union with him)[36] plays such a prominent role in this discussion about the proper formation of the conscience, it is important here briefly to state a few words in its regard. The doctrine of the Church is illumined by Revelation, i.e., what God has revealed to us humans as manifested in His actions with the people of Israel, culminating in Jesus of Nazareth and continuing in the teaching of the Apostles. The contents of the Faith (*fides quae*) of the Church, then, are not something that one gives to oneself or invents or makes up through the free association of ideas and the gathering of information; rather, they are part of a long line of Tradition, i.e., orthodox teaching and practices of divine origin handed on since the time of Christ from generation to generation and from age to age. Likewise, personal faith (*fides qua*) is not something that one gives to oneself—it is not mere conviction—but rather it is a free divine gift. Catholicism, therefore, is not a religious "cafeteria" dispensing doctrine to be chosen ad libitum according to an individual's mood or liking, but rather a coherent and authoritative source of salvation historically traceable to Jesus of Nazareth. Being Catholic, then, presupposes and necessitates an assent and obedience to the authority of God and the Church. The Second Vatican Council succinctly explains:

[33]

Sacred Tradition and Sacred Scripture form one sacred deposit of the word of God, committed to the Church. Holding fast to this deposit the entire holy people united with their shepherds remain always steadfast in the teaching of the Apostles, in the common life, in the breaking of the bread and in prayers,[37] so that holding to, practicing and professing the heritage of the faith, it becomes on the part of the bishops and faithful a single common effort.[38]

But the task of authentically interpreting the word of God, whether written or handed on,[39] has been entrusted exclusively to the living teaching office of the Church,[40] whose authority is exercised in the name of Jesus Christ. This teaching office is not above the word of God, but serves it, teaching only what has been handed on, listening to it devoutly, guarding it scrupulously and explaining it faithfully in accord with a divine commission and with the help of the Holy Spirit, it draws from this one deposit of faith everything which it presents for belief as divinely revealed.

It is clear, therefore, that Sacred Tradition, Sacred Scripture and the teaching authority of the Church, in accord with God's most wise design, are so linked and joined together that one cannot stand without the others, and that all together and each in its own way under the action of the one Holy Spirit contribute effectively to the salvation of souls.[41]

Thus, it is incumbent upon every Catholic to ask honestly if he believes in Revelation and trusts in the authority of God as manifested and safeguarded in the Catholic Church through the historically interwoven triad of Magisterium, Tradition, and Scripture. Simply put, the Catholic must determine if he believes the Church. Without such belief, Catholic Christianity makes little or no sense.

Description of the Conscience and Its Formation

The commonplace understanding of the conscience is that of an individual's freedom of choice on any given matter or issue—or the freedom to be for or against something. Sometimes the conscience is regarded as a personal feeling or sense about what is right or wrong—a gut instinct. While these views on conscience are not entirely off-base, a thematic analysis reveals a more complex and subtle understanding, especially in light of conscience formation.

To begin with, the conscience regards moral action and might be best described as an inner perception (sometimes referred to as the "voice of conscience") of what is good, true, right or just. Working with the intellect and the will, the conscience directs an individual to choose what is good and to avoid what is evil. The conscience serves as a voice of judgment both on an action to be done and on acts already accomplished. The conscience, then, concerns itself in the present with both the future and the past: firstly, on the good to be done here and now and the evil to be avoided; secondly, on the good done or not done and on the evil avoided or not avoided with respect to past actions or omissions. The first gives rise to a reasoned choice on an action to be taken or not; the second to praise or condemnation with regard to decisions of the past.[42] Thus, the *Catechism* states:

> Deep within his conscience man discovers a law which he has not laid upon himself but which he must obey. Its voice, ever calling him to love and to do what is good and to avoid evil, sounds in his heart at the right

moment. . . . For man has in his heart a law inscribed by God. . . . His conscience is man's most secret core and his sanctuary. There he is alone with God whose voice echoes in his depths.[43]

Conscience enables one to assume responsibility for the acts performed. If man commits evil, the just judgment of conscience can remain within him as the witness to the universal truth of the good, at the same time as the evil of his particular choice. The verdict of the judgment of conscience remains a pledge of hope and mercy. In attesting to the fault committed, it calls to mind the forgiveness that must be asked, the good that must still be practiced, and the virtue that must be constantly cultivated with the grace of God.[44]

This activity of the conscience, however, requires proper formation. Here is where the Magisterium of the Church comes in by providing religious and moral instruction on what is good or evil, along with the reasons underlying such determinations. Moreover, the upright example of others, the practice of virtue in daily life, and the Sacraments provide other sources of formation for the conscience.

For Catholics, of particular note for the formation of conscience is the Sacrament of Penance. It is within this Sacrament that an "examination of conscience" is made as an individual reviews or examines his thoughts, words, actions and even omissions in light of the objective moral truth of the Gospel and the contents of the Faith. In fact, this *examen* leads to the "judgment" of the conscience whereby the sinner is moved to confess his sins and failings, to perform acts of penance as reparation for those sins and failings, and to resolve to sin no more.[45] Moreover, frequent reception of the Sacrament of Penance enables one to build a more acute perception of the difference between what is good and evil, oftentimes a high degree of resistance to temptation and thus to sin, and a deeper awareness of God's presence, love, forgiveness and mercy.

The Conscience and Dissent against Church Doctrine

The conscience advises in practical matters, i.e., choices to be made here and now. It does so in favor of the natural moral law, the law of nature,[46] the authoritative teaching of the Magisterium and the laws of the Church as represented in the Bible, the *Catechism*, the Code of Canon Law, etc. In fact, the well-formed conscience informs the rest of the human faculties to adhere to these natural and revealed truths. Hence, Catholics, who have a principled and well-formed conscience, readily assent to biblical and Church teaching to which they willingly conform their actions. In this way, their lives are consistent with their personal act of faith (*fides qua*) and the contents of the Faith of the Church (*fides quae*).

The Congregation for the Doctrine of the Faith (CDF), in its 1990 Instruction *Donum Veritatis*, makes a cogent statement regarding the appeal to one's conscience as an excuse to dissent from Church teaching. Although the document is meant for theologians, its principles are applicable to all Catholics, including politicians who are Catholic. Pertinent to our discussion is the following citation:

> Argumentation appealing to the obligation to follow one's own conscience cannot legitimate dissent. This is true, first of all, because conscience illumines the practical judgment about a decision to make, while here [in matters of faith and morals] we are concerned with the truth of a doctrinal pronouncement. This is furthermore the case because while the theologian, like every

believer, must follow his conscience, he is also obliged
to form it. Conscience is not an independent and infallible faculty. It is an act of moral judgment regarding a
responsible choice. A right conscience is one duly illumined by faith and by the objective moral law and it
presupposes, as well, the uprightness of the will in the
pursuit of the true good.

Setting up a supreme magisterium of conscience in
opposition to the Magisterium of the Church means
adopting a principle of free examination incompatible
with the economy of Revelation and its transmission in
the Church.[47]

The above statement makes the distinction between
judgments of a practical or prudential nature regarding
everyday or typical decisions and judgments of truth concerning matters of faith and morals as taught by the Church.
The former properly relate to the conscience and the latter
to the intellect. For example, the following two questions
are instances of judgments of a practical or prudential nature: Should I buy this car? Should I let my daughter go to a
slumber party at her friend's house? The well-formed conscience enables a reasoned choice in answer to these questions. On the other hand, there are grave issues of a specifically moral nature on which the Church has made conclu-
sive doctrinal pronouncements, such as: Should I get an
abortion? Should I support the manipulation and destruction of human persons through embryonic stem cell "research"? Is it permissible to euthanize a family member?
Should I support same-sex "marriage"? Here, the practical
element remains, but is guided definitively by the
Magisterium. In this way, the intellect, by knowledge of
what the Church teaches, properly informs the conscience
which in turn enables a reasoned choice.

This can be further refined, especially with respect to questions of everyday life or common practical or prudential judgment, which are often open to different options and final decisions. For example: Can I afford this car, given my job or the needs of my family? Do I know the parents of my daughter's friend, and is my daughter going to be safe and taken care of? These two instances could also reveal themselves to have deeper moral consequences: Should I buy this car which I cannot afford, in order to keep up with the lifestyle of my neighbors and as a status symbol for my family? Should I allow my daughter to spend the night at her boyfriend's house? Regarding these types of questions and issues, the *Catechism* instructs:

> The dignity of the human person implies and requires uprightness of moral conscience. Conscience includes the perception of the principles of morality (*synderesis*); their application in the given circumstances by practical discernment of reasons and goods; and finally judgment about concrete acts yet to be performed or already performed. The truth about the moral good, stated in the law of reason, is recognized practically and concretely by the prudent judgment of conscience. We call that man prudent who chooses in conformity with this judgment.[48]

While the Church has not made declarations on *every* specific moral question as the *Catechism* and the two examples above illustrate, Catholicism does provide moral guidance and formation to aid the individual in a reasoned choice. Thus, such particular issues remain open for the individual to choose prudently according to his well-formed conscience: the individual uses his intellect, guided by the natural moral law and by the general moral teaching and principles of the Church, to choose the best course of action here and now.

On the other hand, grave questions regarding the truth of doctrine and moral teaching have necessitated that the Church provide definitive and clear pronouncements. As a consequence, such teaching is no longer open to discussion or different options; an authoritative rational decision in light of the natural law and the Gospel has already been clearly given by the proper authority on such matters: namely, the Magisterium of the Church.[49] Such issues as abortion, euthanasia, embryonic stem cell "research" (which directly destroys innocent humans), and same-sex "marriage" are intrinsically against the natural moral law and, therefore, are always wrong. Church doctrine reflects this natural moral law so that for the Catholic an appeal to his individual conscience cannot legitimate dissent on these and other similar issues. In fact, such an appeal would be erroneous. Thus, when speculation on a particular issue has been removed, the only reasonable choice is that which accords with natural law and magisterial positions. Consequently, the person with a well-formed and upright conscience, trusting in the authority of the Magisterium, recognizes that such issues as abortion, euthanasia, the destruction of human embryos and same-sex "marriage" are unethical and thus either avoids or opposes them.

Of course, the individual always remains, nevertheless, free to choose or to be in favor of such issues. However, such a choice would reflect any combination of the following: a malformed conscience, a lack of moral resolve, poor Christian catechesis, a surrender to temptation or one's passions, a turn toward evil, or possibly a perniciousness rooted in pride or selfishness. Such a choice, with the excuse of appealing to one's own conscience (as many politicians do today), is tantamount to setting up a false and parallel "magisterium of conscience" as the CDF document makes clear. The underdeveloped or poorly-formed conscience (along with a weak will), then, is unable to properly fulfill its function. Furthermore, the conscience can become so poorly-formed or malformed that its voice becomes silenced; its inherent sense of sin is tragically lost therewith, and one's recognition of the distinction between good and evil is blurred. In this regard, Isaiah warns: "Woe to those who call evil good and good evil, who put darkness for light and light for darkness, who put bitter for sweet and sweet for bitter!"[50] Unfortunately, today many people find themselves in such a condition.

The Extrinsic Violation of Conscience

For someone to coerce a Catholic to go against natural moral law or a teaching or a doctrine of the Church would be to force a Catholic to violate his conscience.[51] The Catholic, then, would be in the right and, in actuality, morally obligated, to go against or refuse that which would make him violate Church teaching.[52] The *Catechism* directly addresses this theme:

> The citizen is obliged in conscience not to follow the directives of civil authorities when they are contrary to the demands of the moral order, to the fundamental rights of persons or the teachings of the Gospel. Refusing obedience to civil authorities, when their demands are contrary to those of an upright conscience, finds its justification in the distinction between serving God and serving the political community. "Render therefore to Caesar the things that are Caesar's, and to God the things that are God's."[53] "We must obey God rather than men."[54] "When citizens are under the

oppression of a public authority which oversteps its competence, they should still not refuse to give or to do what is objectively demanded of them by the common good; but it is legitimate for them to defend their own rights and those of their fellow citizens against the abuse of this authority within the limits of the natural law and the Law of the Gospel." [55]

The refusal to submit to such a coercive authority (be it another person, a superior, a government, among others), then, would reflect a well-formed conscience. Hence, as considered earlier, Catholics rightly oppose initiatives such as that of the Department of Health and Human Services' (HHS) mandate on contraceptives, abortifacients and sterilizations, since it disregards chaste sexuality and the sacredness of human life. Furthermore, and this is ultimately the issue, the HHS mandate severely limits the freedom of conscience and the freedom to follow religious beliefs, thereby violating freedom of religion. In this way, the HHS mandate compartmentalizes the life of the believer by limiting what is rendered to God to merely a private act of worship while rendering to Caesar everything else.

While some in the public square may disagree with Catholics on the use of contraceptives, abortifacients and sterilizations, and may not admit their immoral nature, they cannot disagree that the HHS mandate runs against, forces and binds the conscience of Catholics. This is the issue. It is true, societies, at times, hold things which are evil to be good; in that sense, the public square, unfortunately, is not always fully informed by the natural moral law or by the Gospel. Nevertheless, the Catholic is still obligated by the natural moral law and by the Gospel. With the HHS mandate, the problem is precisely the tyrannical overstep of the government onto the conscience of the believer and therefore the proper response of the Catholic is resistance.

II. JFK'S "SPEECH ON FAITH"[56]

Germane to this discussion on conscience is John F. Kennedy, who, as a politician, ironically promoted an arguably anti-Catholic mentality in several of his views on the moral conscience and the role of religion in the public square. He has, of course, subsequently become a prototype for others who have followed his style of Catholicism with regard to public life. His principles on this subject were mainly espoused in a presidential campaign speech to a group of Protestant pastors at the Greater Houston Ministerial Association in 1960 while he was still a senator. Although much could be written both pro and con regarding this "Speech on Faith" or "Ministerial Association Speech," here it is important merely to address two false dichotomies.

False Dichotomy I

In speaking before a group of incredulous Protestant ministers about being a member of the Catholic Church, especially in 1960, it is somewhat understandable that JFK declared the following: "For contrary to common newspaper usage, I am not the Catholic candidate for president. I am the Democratic Party's candidate for president, who happens also to be a Catholic. I do not speak for my Church on public matters, and the Church does not speak for me."[57] He says that he happens to be Catholic because he and forty million other Americans (the number he quotes three paragraphs later)[58] were baptized Catholic. On one level, by quoting the substantial number of Catholics in the United States he is highlighting the importance that he

[43]

is one among a significant demographic and therefore should be respected as such. On a deeper level, however, he is intimating that he is part of a phenomenon known as "cultural Catholicism" wherein an individual is Catholic because he is born into and raised in a family of, for example, Irish, Italian or Hispanic descent. The implication is that an individual as an adult has not yet necessarily fully chosen to be Catholic, which would mean maturely accepting the moral consequences and intellectual theological tradition inherent within Catholic Christianity. So, it is fitting that the future 35th President of the United States make the admission and declare that he is simply a particular party's candidate and not a Catholic candidate for the presidency. He is further correct in saying that the Church does not speak for him on public matters regarding moral issues because his view of the Church, while perhaps sincere, is off-base. Indeed, it is possible to be convinced of possessing a mature faith and its understanding, while in reality the opposite may be the case.

Thus, JFK argues the following with regard to his understanding of the conscience:

> Whatever issue may come before me as president—on birth control, divorce, censorship, gambling or any other subject—I will make my decision in accordance with these views, in accordance with what my conscience tells me to be the national interest, and without regard to outside religious pressures or dictates. And no power or threat of punishment could cause me to decide otherwise.
>
> But if the time should ever come—and I do not concede any conflict to be even remotely possible—when my office would require me to either violate my conscience or violate the national interest, then I

would resign the office; and I hope any conscientious public servant would do the same.[59]

By "these views" mentioned in the first sentence of the quotation above, he is referring to his understanding of the authority of the Church as being non-binding upon Catholic politicians and concomitantly the absolute separation of Church and State as he put forward earlier in preceding paragraphs of this "Ministerial Association Speech." [60] If he were formulating the above first paragraph today, the first part of the first sentence above would read: "Whatever issue may come before me as president—abortion, euthanasia, same-sex 'marriage,' the manipulation and destruction of human embryos for 'research,' etc." Of course, there is no doubt that the second part of the first sentence would still declare: "I will make my decision in accordance with these views, in accordance with what my conscience tells me to be the national interest, and without regard to outside religious pressures or dictates"—in other words, he would have no problem with promoting them all with no regard for Church teaching, the Bishops, or to the "pressures" of denial of the Eucharist or even excommunication. Again, as he says: "I do not speak for my Church on public matters, and the Church does not speak for me." [61]

In this light, it is here that I draw attention to how Senator Kennedy sets up a false dichotomy between his "conscience" and the "national interest" on the one hand and "outside religious pressures or dictates" on the other. It should be noted that the "national interest" does not always equate with the "common good" or with what is right and just. "National interest," in the way that JFK uses it, is code for what the majority of voters wants—what may even be the very vocal but small minority—whom he as a politician is apt to please in order to garner votes and be elected. Of course, what the national majority wants might not always correspond with the supra-national good or the "common good" [62] (for example, take abortion—it is not in children's favor to be defenselessly murdered, but it might be said to be in the "national interest" and therefore of interest to the one who wishes to be elected). Senator Kennedy considers his own conscience to be infallible and compares the national interest with what is right and therefore to be adhered to (not that the national interest is unimportant or always misplaced). In this way, he tries to denominate faith and religion as impositions on his conscience as well as the national interest. By forming this categorization, he or his speechwriter [63] fails to make important distinctions which would connect a well-formed conscience with adherence to the tenets of the Faith, the natural law and the Magisterium of the Church on matters of morals (which truly do affect and effect the national as well as the individual's good).

False Dichotomy II

Perhaps the most notorious and oft-quoted example of Senator Kennedy's miscomprehension of a well-formed conscience and the proper disposition of a person of faith from his "Ministerial Association Speech" is the following statement: "I believe in a president whose religious views are his own private affair, neither imposed by him upon the nation, or imposed by the nation upon him as a condition to holding that office." [64] As we have seen, in stating that it is neither the right of the president nor of the United States to dictate which religion if any to practice, he is correct and in line with the Constitution. However, he sets up once again another false dichotomy this time between "private" and "public" regarding the most important issue in the universe: namely, one's faith or lack of faith in God. JFK's formulation is part of the contemporary wellspring of the "split-person-ality complex" manifested when a politician who is Christian professes to be "personally or privately opposed but publicly for" some gravely immoral issue. Religion as merely a private affair means that one's religious faith has no practical sway on one's thoughts, behaviors or actions. It means that religion does not teach or shape one's character or inform one's decisions. Therefore, according to JFK, in a reference that is thinly-cloaked defiance against the threat of Catholic censure or even the rarely used excommunica-tion, neither God, the Bible nor Christian religious leaders (or any other religious leaders for that matter) have any actual authority: "I believe in an America . . . where no reli-gious body seeks to impose its will directly or indirectly upon the general populace or the public acts of its officials. . . . ."[65] Here, his rhetoric suggests that he is accountable to no moral authority, neither on earth nor in Heaven. While he is correct in that in America, religion is not to be imposed upon the State, he is mistaken to argue that individual Catholics should not be influenced in their decisions by their professed religious views.

Taking the position of JFK from another angle, it is valid to ask about the opposite non-neutral views of belief in a Judeo-Christian God and an accompanying biblical moral-ity, namely: agnosticism, atheism, nihilism, hedonism, an extreme secularism, etc.? Should these be the only views permitted to influence and permeate directly or indirectly the general populace and public officials, as is currently the case? According to Kennedy and so many politicians who have subsequently followed some of his bone-chilling anti-religious rhetoric in his "Speech on Faith," the answer is an obvious "yes." JFK would have us taught that people are to exist in pristine vacuums untouched by systems of belief. The truth is, however, that since the time of childhood, each person is formed for good or for ill by the opinions and attitudes reflective of his parents, relatives, friends, peer group, social status, year of birth, language, ethnicity, religion, education, location, abilities, experiences, etc.—or the lack of some or most of these things. We all have belief systems, some of which are more coherent and better than others; it is part of being human. Thus, it is not to be denied that one's belief or disbelief in God sets the horizons of one's concepts of the nature of humanity, freedom, government and laws. Hence, the need for the formation of the conscience, as noted earlier in this chapter. There is, consequently, no pristine vacuum from which to come nor to which to go. Religion and faith matter. It makes a difference whether one's conscience is formed by the teachings of Jesus of Nazareth or by those of Margaret Sanger—indeed, it is a matter of life or death.[66]

CHAPTER III

Abortion

I. THE NATURE OF ABORTION, AND RELEVANT SOCIETAL ISSUES

An Example of Someone Whose Disposal Abortionists Advised

More than 24 years ago, Pam and her husband Bob were serving as missionaries to the Philippines and praying for a fifth child. Pam contracted amoebic dysentery, an infection of the intestine caused by a parasite found in contaminated food or drink. She went into a coma and was treated with strong antibiotics before they discovered she was pregnant.

Doctors urged her to abort the baby for her own safety and told her that the medicines had caused irreversible damage to her baby. She refused the abortion and cited her Christian faith as the reason for her hope that her son would be born without the devastating disabilities physicians predicted. Pam said the doctors didn't think of it as a life, they thought of it as a mass of fetal tissue.

While pregnant, Pam nearly lost their baby four times but refused to consider abortion. She recalled making a pledge to God with her husband: "If you will give us a son, we'll name him Timothy and we'll make him a preacher."

Pam ultimately spent the last two months of her pregnancy in bed and eventually gave birth to a healthy baby boy on August 14, 1987. Pam's youngest son is indeed a preacher. He preaches in prisons, makes hospital visits, and serves with his father's ministry in the Philippines. He also plays football. Pam's son is Tim Tebow.

The University of Florida's star quarterback became the first sophomore in history to win college football's highest award, the Heisman Trophy. His current role as a quarterback in the National Football League provides an incredible platform for Christian witness.[67]

Biology 101—Nature vs. Public Preference

Building upon what has already been mentioned regarding the immorality of abortion, here it is important to give a more thorough look at this sensitive issue and its consequences. It is helpful at this point to review the stages of pregnancy; for our purposes, it will suffice to focus merely on the biological facts of the first trimester. The following is taken from *MedicineNet.com*, meant as internet educational information for pregnant women:

PREGNANCY is measured in trimesters from the first day of your last menstrual period (LMP) and normally lasts about 40 weeks from conception to the birth of a baby. This time is roughly divided into 3 periods: the first trimester, second trimester and third trimester. The first trimester is measured from conception to about the 12th week of pregnancy; the second trimester, from about 13 to 27 weeks of pregnancy; and the third trimester, from about 28 weeks of pregnancy until birth.

FERTILIZATION: (SPERM PENETRATES EGG) If a sperm cell meets and penetrates an egg, it will fertilize the egg [also known as conception].[68] The fertilization process takes about 24 hours. When fertilization happens, changes occur on the surface of the egg to prevent other sperm from penetrating it. At the moment of fertilization [conception], the genetic makeup is complete, including the sex of the infant.

First Trimester: (Early Changes in a Woman's Body) During the first trimester your body undergoes many changes. Hormonal changes affect almost every organ system in your body. These changes can trigger symptoms even in the very first weeks of pregnancy. Your period stopping is a clear sign that you are pregnant.

First Trimester: (The Baby [by] 4 Weeks) Your baby's brain and spinal cord have begun to form. The heart begins to form. Arm and leg buds appear. Your baby is now an embryo[69] and 1/25 of an inch long.

First Trimester: (The Baby [by] 8 Weeks) All major organs and external body structures have begun to form. Your baby's heart beats with a regular rhythm. The arms and legs grow longer, and fingers and toes have begun to form. The sex organs begin to form. The eyes have moved forward on the face and eyelids have formed. The umbilical cord is clearly visible. At the end of 8 weeks, your baby is a fetus and looks more like a human. Your baby is nearly 1 inch long and weighs less than 1/8 of an ounce.

First Trimester: (The Baby [by] 12 Weeks) The nerves and muscles begin to work together. Your baby can make a fist. The external sex organs show if your baby is a boy or girl. A woman who has an ultrasound in the second trimester or later might be able to find out the baby's sex. Eyelids close to protect the developing eyes. They will not open again until the 28th week.

Head growth has slowed, and your baby is much longer. Now, at about 3 inches long, your baby weighs almost an ounce.[70]

Probably the most important words from the above description are: "At the moment of fertilization [conception], the genetic makeup is complete, including the sex of the infant." As basic biology explains, then, at the moment of conception the human person[71] in his entirety is present. In this regard, the Church teaches that every human person has an inherit equality and transcendent value and it does not matter at which stage of development that human person might be.[72] For Catholics, it makes no sense, therefore, that another human person (be one a physician or abortionist or even the person's mother) should be able to end a new human person's life. We were all once in our mother's womb. For anyone who claims to be decent, not only should killing another innocent human person be illegal; it should be unthinkable. Murder is not health care nor should it be described as a "preventive service."

Pope Benedict XVI, in his address to the German Parliament in September of 2011, made the following distinction: "For most of the matters that need to be regulated by law, the support of the majority can serve as a sufficient criterion. Yet it is evident that for the fundamental issues of law, in which the dignity of man and of humanity is at stake, the majority principle is not enough."[73] Phil Lawler of *CatholicCulture.org*, commenting on the Holy Father's statement, makes the following observation:

A popular vote is a wonderful way to settle questions about public preferences. But not all questions can be settled in the same way. As Pope Benedict recently reminded the Bundestag, basic human rights cannot be subject to the passing whims of popularity, and thus "it is evident that for the fundamental issues of law, in which the dignity of man and of humanity is at stake, the majority principle is not enough." The Pope went on to explain that the most essential human rights are innate: permanently encoded in human nature. These rights are expressed in the natural law, whose authority is both prior and superior to any man-made law.[74]

The natural law is the reflection of the divine law, i.e., the reasoned ordering of created reality willed by God. The natural law "enables man to discern by reason the good and the evil, the truth and the lie."[75] It "governs man's moral life" by directing his moral choices toward this order of reality such that true happiness, goodness and perfection might be attained.[76] Civil, or positive law, to be just, must reflect the natural law.[77] In this way, we could say that the natural law directs the moral choices of man much as the laws of nature or science bind creation. Thus, the natural law builds upon the law of nature: Human life begins at conception—which is universally true of all of us and is basic biology and has now become scientifically verifiable by modern technology. Consequently, the natural law reflects the order of nature and teaches that an unborn child is a person and has basic human rights which are inviolable.[78] Among those basic human rights is preeminently the right to live. Extinguishing an innocent human life, then, cannot be a matter of political opinion. The right to life is not a preference, a policy, nor a legislative procedure open to a minority or a majority vote. Rather, the protection of innocent life is a political duty. In that light, the landmark 1973 Supreme Court decision (*Roe v. Wade*) should never have occurred since it is morally unconscionable that an innocent human life could ever be taken and sanctioned by laws brought about by legislation or by a court of nine judges.

Even in instances of a child conceived as a result of rape, as deplorable as the crime against the woman is, an abortion is not the solution. The woman, while physically and psychologically violated, still has her life with the ability of rehabilitation. The unborn child's life, however, through an abortion is taken away with no possibility of recovery. Also, from a psychological point of view, an abortion in the case of rape could be looked upon as a means of "covering over" or "masking," instead of identifying and healing the real wounds caused by the violation. This does not even begin to consider the many other psychological complexes which affect a woman after she has had an abortion (but more on this later in the chapter).

The Number of Abortions, and the Highly Profitable Abortion Industry

According to the Planned Parenthood Federation of America's (PPFA's) most recent annual report (July 1, 2009—June 30, 2010), its clinics performed 329,455 abortions and received in "government health services grants and reimbursements" (otherwise known as tax-payers' money) $487.4 million.[79] Although tax-payer money cannot be used legally to pay directly for abortions, when monies are given to agencies (like Planned Parenthood) which provide abortions, it can be used to pay for the clinics, the personnel, the instruments employed in performing an abortion, etc. So, when tax money goes to such organizations, the tax-payer is helping indirectly to fund abortions, along with the many other immoral things they do: contributing to hedonism and moral relativism, providing contraceptives, promoting pornography and unrestrained sex through "education" programs, etc.[80]

According to the PPFA's website, an in-clinic abortion procedure in the first trimester costs between $300 and $950.[81] In addition, the website states: "The cost is usually more for a second-trimester abortion. Costs vary depending on how long you've been pregnant and where you go. Hospitals generally cost more."[82] The numbers for the fiscal year 2009-2010 are: 329,455 x $300 = $98,836,500 or 329,455 x $950 = $312,982,250. In other words, Planned Parenthood's revenue just from abortions is between $98,836,500 and $312,982,250. According to another pro-abortion entity, the Guttmacher Institute, "in 2009, the average amount paid for a nonhospital abortion with local anesthesia at 10 weeks' gestation was $451."[83] Here the numbers are: 329,455 x $451 = $148,584,205. Also, according to the Guttmacher Institute, it is estimated that annually 1,210,000 abortions are performed in the United States through the various abortion agencies and providers.[84] So, 1,210,000 x $451 = $545,710,000 in revenue—just in the US alone from the murder of innocent humans through surgically-induced abortions. If one adds the revenue from chemical abortive drugs (abortifacients such as the Morning After Pill, Ella, RU-486),[85] the profits of this industry skyrocket.[86] Abortion is evidently big business.

Protecting the Life of the Woman

An argument often raised by pro-abortionists is that providing women legal access to abortion saves countless lives of women. In the United States, with the advances in medicine and the use of penicillin and antibiotics, that is simply not true. Already in 1960, a former medical director of Planned Parenthood, Mary Calderone, speaking of abortions performed in the United States, made the following declaration:

> Abortion is no longer a dangerous procedure. This applies not just to therapeutic abortions as performed in hospitals but also to so-called illegal abortions as done by physician. In 1957 there were only 260 deaths in the whole country attributed to abortions of any kind. . . . Whatever trouble arises usually arises from self-induced abortions, which comprise approximately 8 percent, or with the very small percentage that go to some kind of non-medical abortionist. . . . Abortion, whether therapeutic or illegal, is in the main no longer dangerous. . . .[87]

Currently, it is estimated that every year fewer than fifty women in the United States would be at risk of death by non-professional abortion procedures.[88] It is obvious that such a number pales in comparison with 1,210,000 innocent babies who are exterminated annually in the United States because of legalized abortion. Another consideration is that those women would be choosing an abortion and the risks associated with it, whereas the 1,210,000 unborn would have no say in preserving their life.

Here, it is warranted merely to point out two internal flaws in the rhetoric and logic of abortion as "safe, legal, and rare." First, why would a non-harmful and health-promoting or disease-preventing legal procedure need to be rare? Second, it is obvious that abortion is never safe for the child.

How Abortions Are Performed: The Philadelphia Example

The deliberate destruction of innocent human life is abnormal and irrational. If a doctor or licensed medical technician has no problem of conscience with performing early-stage abortions, it should be asked then why would such an individual have a problem with late-term and partial-birth abortions or even infanticide? An example of a "doctor" who feels no moral compunction to stop killing at any stage is Dr. Kermit Gosnell of Philadelphia.

Gosnell faces eight counts of murder in the deaths of a woman following a botched abortion at his office, along with the deaths of seven babies who, prosecutors allege, were born alive following illegal late-term abortions and were then killed with scissors, reports CBS affiliate KYW./ Gosnell, 69, made millions of dollars over 30 years, performing as many illegal, late-term abortions as he could, prosecutors said. State regulators ignored complaints about him and failed to visit or inspect his clinic since 1993, but no charges were warranted against them, District Attorney Seth Williams said. / Gosnell "induced labor, forced the live birth of viable babies in the sixth, seventh, eighth month of pregnancy and then killed those babies by cutting into the back of the neck with scissors and severing their spinal cord," Williams said.[89]

Repugnant, but who is to regulate an abortionist and the highly lucrative abortion industry? This scenario merely exemplifies the procedure of every abortion: innocent humans are inhumanely destroyed by culpable adults under the guise of a "medical procedure." That said, it is not certain what marks out Gosnell from any other abortionist and why even for pro-abortion advocates his actions are condemned and even considered illegal. After all, the differences between a person just beginning to grow in the womb and a person in the third trimester are merely size and development of capacities: as biology demonstrates, human life is there from conception.

Abortion as an "Act of Love"?

In a recent interview, the Queens, New York, abortion clinic operator and career "pro-choice" activist Merle Hoffman advocates for the further destygmatization of abortion in society. The interview records Hoffman as having no qualms about admitting that an abortion destroys an innocent human life:

> Interestingly, although the standard pro-choice line is essentially to let the woman define the embryo or fetus for herself, Hoffman has a more controversial stance: "In the beginning they [pro-lifers] were calling it a baby. We [pro-abortionists] were saying it was only blood and tissue. Let's agree this is a life form, a potential life; you're terminating it. You don't have to argue that abortion stops a beating heart. It does." She adds, "I can't say it's just like an appendectomy. It isn't. It's a very powerful and loaded decision." [90]

Moreover, Hoffman claims that having an abortion is an act of love and an affirmation of motherhood:

> She also writes about her own abortion, which occurred after she'd been running the clinic for several years. . . . "With my choice I was fighting for the right of all women to define abortion as an act of love: love for the family one already has, and just as important, love for oneself. I was fighting to reclaim abortion as a mother's act. It was an act of solidarity as significant as any other I had committed." [91]

[58]

Merle Hoffman (and all who might think the way she does) is tragically misguided in advocating a notion of autonomy, self-expression, self-determination and self-fulfillment at the costly expense of the destruction of another human and under the rubric of being "pro-choice." To kill one's own unborn child and possibly to view such a killing as an act of maternal love and solidarity turns logic and the meaning of motherhood upside down. This reductionist attitude and attempt at self-justification merely serve to empty the human person of value, rationality and above all the capacity to love and to be loved. What Merle Hoffman needs is the grace to recognize the gravity of what she has done (and continues to advocate) with an accompanying repentance, self-forgiveness, and healing.

The Aftershock of an Abortion

Believe it or not, there are some abortion advocates who claim that having an abortion is psychologically beneficial. It is common practice to justify an abortion by citing claims that the procedure will improve the mental health of the woman. A recent study done in the United Kingdom, however, debunks such a theory.[92] In an interview, Peter Saunders, MD, states:

"This new review shows that abortion does not improve mental health outcomes for women with unplanned pregnancies, despite 98% of the 200,000 abortions being carried out in this country [the UK] each year on mental health grounds./ This means that when doctors authorize abortions in order to protect a woman's mental health they are doing so on the basis of a false belief not supported by the medical evidence." [93]

In counter-distinction to the improvement point of view, there are significant studies and testimonies which draw a relation between abortion and residual psychological and emotional scars of the procedure on women (and sometimes on complicit men).[94] The already-mentioned Mary Calderone, a former medical director of Planned Parenthood, of all people wrote in this regard:

> I ask you not to assume that I am indiscriminately for abortion. Believe me, I am not. Aside from the fact that abortion is the taking of a life, I am also mindful of what was brought out by our psychiatrists that in almost every case, abortion, whether legal or illegal, is a traumatic experience that may have severe consequences later on./ There was general agreement with the words of one psychiatrist: "When a responsible female seeks an abortion, unless the warrant for it is overwhelming as say in the case of rape or incest we are in effect confronted both with a sick person and a sick situation."[95]

In addition, the trauma of an abortion which she acknowledges has been known to cause or contribute to such conditions as the following: clinical depression, chronic feelings of guilt, suicide, drinking and drug use, nightmares, flash-backs, insomnia, and even anniversary reactions.[96] While these effects are not the essential reason for the immoral nature of an abortion, they do confirm its evil consequences. In this context, it is to be noted that there are several excellent programs available (such as Project Rachel[97] and Rachel's Vineyard[98]) which assist women who have had abortions, are grieving their loss, and are psychologically coping.

Abortion Promotion and "Gender Equality"

A 2012 statement of President Barack Obama raises another important issue now to be considered.

> As we mark the 39th anniversary of Roe v. Wade, we must remember that this Supreme Court decision not only protects a woman's health and reproductive freedom, but also affirms a broader principle: that government should not intrude on private family matters. I remain committed to protecting a woman's right to choose and this fundamental constitutional right. While this is a sensitive and often divisive issue—no matter what our views, we must stay united in our determination to prevent unintended pregnancies, support pregnant woman and mothers, reduce the need for abortion, encourage healthy relationships, and promote adoption. And as we remember this historic anniversary, we must also continue our efforts to ensure that our daughters have the same rights, freedoms, and opportunities as our sons to fulfill their dreams.[99]

Notwithstanding the pretentious rhetoric of this statement, the issue that concerns us here is that of the last sentence. The Catholic Church acknowledges that all people are equal and have an inherent dignity. The Catholic Church, however, does not deny that there is an anatomical difference between male and female and, therefore, accompanying consequences. Males and females do share the same rights and freedoms; however, when it comes to the opportunities and the fulfillment of personal goals and dreams that the presidential statement mentions, the anatomical difference ineluctably comes into play.

[61]

It is not naturally possible for a male to be pregnant and carry a child. That opportunity and gift of nature and the bond between a mother and her child, due to anatomy and the law of nature (meaning true to the nature of the way that things are set up), are not given to males. While the capacity to bear children is an opportunity for females that males do not have, it is also a responsibility reserved to females that males do not share in, except vicariously and volitionally. This is no small difference between the two sexes as this distinction has an impact on how careers and dreams are fulfilled. A woman's life trajectory is singularly determined by this capacity, whereas a man's life trajectory is determined by child-bearing only to the extent to which he chooses to participate. The advocates of abortion and so-called "gender equality," in denying this fact of life which is known to all, are inauthentic, untruthful and insincere concerning the most basic level of human existence.

Abortion, then, seen through the lens of the Obama Administration, is, in reality, aggressive social engineering through the technological manipulation of the female in order to compensate for a perceived inequality in the natural distinction between the two sexes. The male and the female need to be viewed correctly: as being in complementarity with one another and therefore as the fulfillment of each other and the culmination of each other's deepest desires, aspirations and dreams through mutual creative love open to the gift of a child. The abortion mindset, however, pits females and males against each other and, in point of fact, in competition. To abort an innocent child so that one's own dreams might be fulfilled is selfish and immoral and should not be protected by government and laws. To revert to contraception and abortion and to create and promote a general contraceptive and abortive mentality is not only unchristian, it is inhumane. It erodes the human family and the very fabric of society. Actions have consequences, which is why for the Catholic chaste sexual activity takes place within the context of marriage where the wife and husband responsibly and accountably welcome their offspring as a gift and blessing. Sexual activity, limited to the confines of marriage, is not only reflective of morality, it is good public policy with enormous benefits to society as a whole. In the end, on every level, the abortion worldview is tragic and destructive.

Testimony and Conversion of Former Pro-Abortionists

In the Gospel of John, Jesus proclaims that "the thief comes only to steal and kill and destroy. I came that [you] may have life, and have it abundantly." [100] Jesus is the "way, and the truth and the life," [101] and there is a growing number of eloquent testimonies of former pro-abortionists and their conversion to Christianity through the pro-life movement. Here I will make note of only two.

Norma McCorvey was plaintiff Jane Roe in the 1973 lawsuit *Roe v. Wade*, which legalized abortion in the United States. She writes:

> I could out-cuss the most crass of men and women; I could out-drink many of the Dallas taverns' regulars; and I was known for my hot temper. When pro-lifers called me a murderer, I called them worse. When people held up signs of aborted fetuses, I spit in their face./ I had a reputation to protect, after all. As the plaintiff in the infamous Supreme Court case Roe v. Wade, my life was inextricably tied up with abortion. Though I had never had one, abortion was the sun around which my life orbited. I once told a reporter,

[63]

"This issue is the only thing I live for. I live, eat, breathe, think everything about abortion."[102]

Over the course of time and through the persistence of a local pro-life group, she went from the above attitude to becoming a Christian:

When my conversion became public knowledge, I spoke openly to reporters about still supporting legalized abortion in the first trimester. The media was quick to use this to downplay the seriousness of my conversion, saying I typified the "general ambivalence" of our culture over abortion. But a few weeks after my conversion, I was sitting in Operation Rescue's offices when I noticed a fetal development poster. The progression was so obvious, the eyes were so sweet. It hurt my heart, just looking at them.

I ran outside and finally, it dawned on me. "Norma," I said to myself, "They're right." I had worked with pregnant women for years. I had been through three pregnancies and deliveries myself. I should have known. Yet something in that poster made me lose my breath. I kept seeing the picture of that tiny, 10-week-old embryo, and I said to myself, that's a baby! It's as if blinders just fell off my eyes and I suddenly understood the truth—that's a baby!

I felt "crushed" under the truth of this realization. I had to face up to the awful reality. Abortion wasn't about "products of conception." It wasn't about "missed periods." It was about children being killed in their mothers' wombs. All those years I was wrong. Signing that affidavit, I was wrong. Working in an abortion clinic, I was wrong. No more of this first trimester, second trimester, third trimester stuff. Abortion—at any point—was wrong. It was so clear. Painfully clear.[103]

Today, she is a practicing Catholic and has her own pro-life apostolate with the mission of overturning *Roe v. Wade*.

Another profound conversion is that of the late Bernard Nathanson. He was one of the original founders of the National Abortion Rights Action League (NARAL Pro-Choice America) in 1968.[104] It was through his efforts that abortion was legalized in the United States and throughout his career as an abortionist he was personally responsible for performing 75,000 abortions.[105] However, he went from that pro-abortion record to becoming a pro-life advocate and even exposing the tactics that the abortion lobbyists use to gain recognition: capturing the media, vilifying the Catholic hierarchy and teachings, and suppressing the scientific evidence that life begins at conception.[106] After his conversion, he wrote:

> I am often asked what made me change my mind. How did I change from prominent abortionist to pro-life advocate? In 1973, I became director of obstetrics of a large hospital in New York City and had to set up a prenatal research unit, just at the start of a great new technology which we now use every day to study the fetus in the womb. A favorite pro-abortion tactic is to insist that the definition of when life begins is impossible; that the question is a theological or moral or philosophical one, anything but a scientific one. Fetology makes it undeniably evident that life begins at conception and requires all the protection and safeguards that any of us enjoy. Why, you may well ask, do

some American doctors who are privy to the findings of fetology, discredit themselves by carrying out abortions? Simple arithmetic at $300 a time, 1.55 million abortions means an industry generating $500,000,000 annually, of which most goes into the pocket of the physician doing the abortion. It is clear that permissive abortion is purposeful destruction of what is undeniably human life. It is an impermissible act of deadly violence. One must concede that unplanned pregnancy is a wrenchingly difficult dilemma, but to look for its solution in a deliberate act of destruction is to trash the vast resourcefulness of human ingenuity, and to surrender the public weal to the classic utilitarian answer to social problems.[107]

On February 21, 2011, Bernard Nathanson died a faithful Catholic; and his funeral Mass was held at St. Patrick's Cathedral in New York.

How Can We Help?

There is also a further consideration that needs to be addressed: Although there are programs already in place in many dioceses to aid a woman who is struggling with a pregnancy, the Catholic community (among other religious and social-oriented agencies) could do much more on a practical level to restore a culture of life and to combat the destructive culture of death which abortion promotes. Girls in middle or high school, young women in college, other women either single or married but nonetheless in difficult, unstable or abusive relationships, face an enormous challenge when they are pregnant. The young girl or the woman who is pregnant needs to be helped in a practical manner so as to inspire hope in her and so that she might not cave into the societal pressure (or that of the abortion industry) to have an abortion.

The practical ways of helping this type of woman could be: (1) counseling—a pregnancy is not the end of the world (ask Justin Bieber's mom: single, low-income, age eighteen) and life (both the mother's and her child's) will go on; (2) emotional assistance: She needs to know that someone authentically cares about her and her situation and that she can trust and confide in someone; (3) in many cases, she needs to be financially assisted: How is she going to be financially provided for if she has her child? If she is in college and lives in a dormitory or an apartment, has a roommate and pays rent, her studies are going to be affected and so how are the changes of having a child going to be accounted for? As Catholics, we must step up and let it be known that we are willing and able to help. As the Apostle James writes: "Faith of itself, if it does not have works, is dead." [108]

II. ABORTION AND CAPITAL PUNISHMENT

It is often said that to be truly pro-life, one must not only be against abortion, but also against the death penalty. This stance is reflective of an "absolutist" position which argues that capital punishment is always wrong inasmuch as a human life is taken. [109] Those who are against abortion but are for the use of capital punishment, then, are made out to be hypocrites. However, this position, for various reasons, is untenable as foreseen in Catholic moral theology.

Although the issues of abortion and capital punishment are related, they are in reality very different. [110] They are related in that both concern human life; however, they regard human life in radically distinct ways. Abortion involves the direct taking of an innocent human life. The death penalty, on the other hand, while it is the direct taking of a human life, is a form of *justice* which deals with the crime and consequent punishment of someone who is guilty (assuming that the culpability has been proven).

In an article entitled "Catholicism and Capital Punishment," the late Cardinal Dulles wrote:

> Summarizing the verdict of Scripture and tradition, we can glean some settled points of doctrine. It is agreed that crime deserves punishment in this life and not only in the next. In addition, it is agreed that the State has authority to administer appropriate punishment to those judged guilty of crimes and that this punishment may, in serious cases, include the sentence of death.[111]

From a teleological analysis, according to Cardinal Dulles, criminal punishment has at least four ends or goals: rehabilitation, defense against the criminal, deterrence, and retribution. After examining each goal, he states:

> The death penalty, we may conclude, has different values in relation to each of the four ends of punishment. It does not rehabilitate the criminal but may be an occasion for bringing about salutary repentance. It is an effective but rarely, if ever, a necessary means of defending society against the criminal. Whether it serves to deter others from similar crimes is a disputed question, difficult to settle. Its retributive value is impaired by lack of clarity about the role of the State. In general, then, capital punishment has some limited value but its necessity is open to doubt.[112]

Capital punishment, in extreme circumstances, then, both on the levels of theory and practical prudence, could be warranted, provided that it is carried out as a matter of justice (and not revenge or vendetta). The *Catechism* further elaborates:

> "Human life is sacred because from its beginning it involves the creative action of God and it remains forever in a special relationship with the Creator, who is its sole end. God alone is the Lord of life from its beginning until its end: no one can under any circumstance claim for himself the right directly to destroy an *innocent* human being [emphasis added]." [113]
>
> Assuming that the guilty party's identity and responsibility have been fully determined, the traditional teaching of the Church does not exclude recourse to the death penalty, if this is the only possible way of effectively defending human lives against the unjust aggressor./ If, however, non-lethal means are sufficient to defend and protect people's safety from the aggressor, authority will limit itself to such means, as these are more in keeping with the concrete conditions of the common good and more in conformity to the dignity of the human person./ Today, in fact, as a consequence of the possibilities which the state has for effectively preventing crime, by rendering one who has committed an offense incapable of doing harm without definitely taking away from him the possibility of redeeming himself the cases in which the execution of the offender is an absolute necessity "are very rare, if not practically nonexistent." [114]

Therefore, with an understanding of the modern State's ability to employ other effective means to contain persons who have committed grave crimes or who are considered dangerous, thereby protecting society at large, capital punishment, although not absolutely prohibited, should be used very seldom, if ever.

There is still another misconception regarding the issues of abortion and capital punishment. Some people consider the State's use of the death penalty to be as common as abortion; however, in actuality, there is a vast disparity between the two. Since 1976, there have been a total of 1,279 recourses to the death penalty in the United States.[115] That number represents approximately 35 deaths per year. On the other hand, since 1973, the number of murders of innocent human life through directly-induced abortions is over 50,000,000 or approximately 1,210,000 per year (and that number does not take into consideration the number of chemical abortions by the recent abortifacients).[116] Consequently, even numerically, there is no equivalence between these two issues. This numerical comparison is not an argument, but simply a statement of facts.

In conclusion, to compare abortion and the death penalty and those who are in favor of either the one or the other is unreasonable. Although to be pro-life means to be pro-every-human life (whether the innocent unborn or the guilty murderer in prison), as has been shown, there are fundamental differences between advocating abortion and supporting capital punishment. Abortion truly is a *life issue* whereas capital punishment is, in reality, an *issue of justice* in the modern State.

CHAPTER IV

Marriage and Its Pretenders

I. CHURCH TEACHING REGARDING SEXUALITY AND MARRIAGE

The discussion of same-sex issues is sensitive and complex. The legalization of same-sex relationships is often presented as a solution to anxieties and crises experienced by a particular group of people within society due to their life circumstances and behavior. On the other hand, the attempt to legalize relationships between same-sex couples for the institution of *marriage* has become a means to force social acceptance of same-sex attraction and relationships on society-at-large.

Nevertheless, there is a clear distinction between couples of the opposite sex and those of the same-sex, and there are important and obvious reasons why the institution of marriage is reserved exclusively for two people of the opposite sex. There are also reasons why a putative same-sex "marriage" is neither a fundamental (or basic) human right nor a civil right. Furthermore, the Catholic Church's understanding of marriage is objective and just. This chapter will support these theses by means of both a theological and a philosophical way of argumentation and will substantiate the claim that the Catholic should vote for marriage between one man and one woman and for candidates who support the Defense of Marriage Act (DOMA).

The Bible and Homosexuality

According to the *Catechism of the Catholic Church*, Scripture "presents homosexual acts as acts of grave depravity." [117]

The following biblical verses are cited in the footnote of the *Catechism*'s number 2357: Gen 19:1-29; Rom 1:24-27; 1 Cor 6:10; 1 Tim 1:10. Genesis 19:1-29 is a depiction of the ancient towns of Sodom and Gomor'rah, which were notoriously destroyed because of their immorality and homosexuality.[118] One might note that the English words sodomy and sodomite come from this text from the Book of Genesis. Regarding the New Testament, Saint Paul, in his epistles, strictly forbids same-sex behaviors and considers them immoral:

ROMANS 1:24-27: Therefore God gave them up in the lusts of their hearts to impurity, to the dishonoring of their bodies among themselves, because they exchanged the truth about God for a lie and worshiped and served the creature rather than the Creator, who is blessed forever! Amen. For this reason God gave them up to dishonorable passions. Their women exchanged natural relations for unnatural, and the men likewise gave up natural relations with women and were consumed with passion for one another, men committing shameless acts with men and receiving in their own persons the due penalty for their error.

1 CORINTHIANS 6:9-11: Do you not know that the unrighteous will not inherit the kingdom of God? Do not be deceived; neither the immoral, nor idolaters, nor adulterers, nor sexual perverts, nor thieves, nor the greedy, nor drunkards, nor revilers, nor robbers will inherit the kingdom of God. And such were some of you. But you were washed, you were sanctified, you were justified in the name of the Lord Jesus Christ and in the Spirit of our God.

1 TIMOTHY 1:5-11: Whereas the aim of our charge is love that issues from a pure heart and a good conscience and sincere faith. Certain persons by swerving from these have wandered away into vain discussion, desiring to be teachers of the law, without understanding either what they are say-

ing or the things about which they make assertions. Now we know that the law is good, if any one uses it lawfully, understanding this, that the law is not laid down for the just but for the lawless and disobedient, for the ungodly and sinners, for the unholy and profane, for murderers of fathers and murderers of mothers, for manslayers, immoral persons, sodomites, kidnapers, liars, perjurers, and whatever else is contrary to sound doctrine, in accordance with the glorious gospel of the blessed God with which I have been entrusted.[119]

Although these passages are not exhaustive, they exemplify that the Old and New Testaments serve as the revealed foundation of the Church's teaching on homosexuality, particularly on the immorality of homosexual behavior. In addition, this teaching is founded upon the Church's understanding of the natural moral law. This becomes apparent when we turn to the *Catechism* itself.

The Catechism *and Homosexuality*

The *Catechism of the Catholic Church* speaks directly on the issue of homosexuality in terms of the natural moral law and the law of nature in its section entitled "Chastity and Homosexuality." The three paragraphs are cited here in full:

> 2357: Homosexuality refers to relations between men or between women who experience an exclusive or predominant sexual attraction toward persons of the same sex. It has taken a great variety of forms through the centuries and in different cultures. Its psychological genesis remains largely unexplained. Basing itself on Sacred Scripture, which presents homosexual acts as acts of grave depravity, tradition has always declared that "homosexual acts are intrinsically disordered."[120]

They are contrary to the natural law. They close the sexual act to the gift of life. They do not proceed from a genuine affective and sexual complementarity. Under no circumstances can they be approved.

2358: The number of men and women who have deep-seated homosexual tendencies is not negligible. This inclination, which is objectively disordered, constitutes for most of them a trial. They must be accepted with respect, compassion, and sensitivity. Every sign of unjust discrimination in their regard should be avoided. These persons are called to fulfill God's will in their lives and, if they are Christians, to unite to the sacrifice of the Lord's Cross the difficulties they may encounter from their condition.

2359: Homosexual persons are called to chastity. By the virtues of self-mastery that teach them inner freedom, at times by the support of disinterested friendship, by prayer and sacramental grace, they can and should gradually and resolutely approach Christian perfection.

In this light, the Catholic Church makes a distinction between living in a same sex relationship (homosexuality) and being attracted to the same sex. Homosexuality and living the "gay lifestyle" are disordered and immoral in and of themselves. Same-sex attraction, while it is disordered, is not immoral because immorality deals with actions and behaviors—choices—while an inclination or attraction does not necessarily have to be acted upon. Catholics, then, do not turn away or reject those who describe themselves as being attracted to the same sex. There is a percentage of the members of the Church which is same-sex attracted and these people enjoy the "gift of faith" and believe in Jesus as Lord and Savior. For them, although they be attracted to persons of the same sex, the legalization of same-sex "marriage" and the promotion of a gay "culture" or "lifestyle" would be the farthest things from their wishes and desires. In fact, on account of their love for Jesus and the Church and in their own personal witness to holiness, they are not in same-sex relationships. Some even actively campaign against attempts at same-sex "marriage."

The following questions might then be posed—and answered.

—Is the disordered inclination or attraction to a person of the same sex sinful in and of itself? No.

—Is the person of same-sex attraction able to be saved and be described as a "child of God?" Yes.

—Is the person with these inclinations capable of virtue and holiness? Yes.

—Is it also possible that this person be a person of great moral integrity? Yes.

All people are called to know and love Jesus. It is the Church's mission as the Body of Christ, the ambassador of Christ and as Christ's unique sacramental presence on earth, to announce this message and make it possible. Each person is endowed with a transcendent value and has an inherent equality, whether he be attracted to the same sex or to the opposite sex.[121] This is "good news."

Church Teaching on Chastity and Marriage

Standards of sexual morality and intimacy are derived from the constant teachings of the Catholic Church from the time of Jesus and as depicted in the Bible. Illustrative in this regard is Jesus' own commentary on the sixth of the Ten Commandments as recorded in the Gospel of Matthew: "You have heard that it was said, 'You shall not commit adultery.' But I say to you that every one who looks at a woman lustfully has already committed adultery with her in his heart." [122]

It might be asked: "Who can bear such teaching?" The passage not only rules out lust and adultery, but also (as elsewhere in the Holy Scriptures) pornography, masturbation, fornication, cohabitation, prostitution, incest and rape. [123] Furthermore, willful expression of genital activity outside of marriage contradicts Church teaching and is sinful. This instruction regards all persons who are not married, whether they be male or female, with same-sex or opposite-sex attractions. With this understanding, genital sexual expression is exclusive and proper only to those joined legitimately in marriage. The *Catechism* explains:

Sexuality is ordered to the conjugal love of man and woman. In marriage the physical intimacy of the spouses becomes a sign and pledge of spiritual communion. Marriage bonds between baptized persons are sanctified by the sacrament. [124]

Sexuality, by means of which man and woman give themselves to one another through the acts which are proper and exclusive to spouses, is not something simply biological, but concerns the innermost being of the human person as such. It is realized in a truly human way only if it is an integral part of the love by which a man and woman commit themselves totally to one another until death. . . . [125]

The acts in marriage by which the intimate and chaste union of the spouses takes place are noble and honorable; the truly human performance of these acts fosters the self-giving they signify and enriches the spouses in joy and gratitude. [126] Sexuality is a source of joy and pleasure. . . . [127]

The spouses' union achieves the twofold end of

marriage: the good of the spouses themselves and the transmission of life. These two meanings or values of marriage cannot be separated without altering the couple's spiritual life and compromising the goods of marriage and the future of the family. The conjugal love of man and woman thus stands under the twofold obligation of fidelity and fecundity.[128]

It is important to take note of the interconnected triad of conjugality (the good of the spouses), faithfulness and open-ness to life. From this intimate union of life and love, the basic unit of society is constituted and protected and, thereby, the common good and flourishing of society itself. Once again, the importance of the natural moral law can be observed in the teaching of the Church.

II. A TECHNICAL ANALYSIS OF ORDER AND COMPLEMENTARITY

The Non-Professionalism of the "Professionals"

People do not like to be told that they are sick, diseased or, what is more, that they are disordered. Up until the "sexual revolution" of the 1960's and 1970's, homosexuality was still classified as a pathological disorder, i.e., a disease, by the major different psychiatric and psychological associations (including the APA until 1973).[129] Now, however, homo-sexuality has been declassified as such. Thus, as Catholics, it is difficult to take mainstream medical journals seriously when they speak of homosexuality as not being a disorder.[130] Moreover, in my research, it was difficult to find an article on the non-disordered nature of homosexuality which was written without including social value judgments. Does this not reveal a political agenda to "normalize" these behav-iors? Medscape Reference is merely one example among many which warrants a positive response to this question. It states the following:

> Homosexuality is not a medical or psychiatric disorder, but is a condition associated with certain medical risks. Homosexuality has long been recognized both in human and animal populations. Despite the relative frequency of homosexuality, it remains misunderstood and controversial to much of society. Homosexual individuals who choose members of their own sex for sexual relations and domestic partnerships are often targets of prejudice and may even be discriminated against by health care professionals.
>
> On the societal level in the United States, each person is usually understood as being either gay or straight, and there is little notice given to the bisexual or others of various gradations in sexual preference. For example, many military, religious, educational, and voluntary organizations often demonstrate intense interest in whether one of their members is or is not homosexual, and they determine ways to deal with the individual once this label has been applied. The intent is usually to expel, or in some way marginalize, the homosexual individual.
>
> Again, importantly, homosexuality is not a psychiatric disorder. In this section, the authors briefly review psychiatric disorders that involve elements of sexuality and that could be confused with homosexuality. The purpose of this discussion is to differentiate these disorders from homosexuality and to refer readers to other *eMedicine* articles for further discussion.[131]

As is evident, the agenda in the article, and I would hazard to say most of the articles which do not classify same-sex attraction and activity as disordered, is to hammer home that there is nothing morally wrong with homosexuality and the gay lifestyle, that same-sex couples should be accepted by everyone and everywhere, and that those who have a problem with them (often mentioned are the religiously minded) are intolerant bigots.[132] These are supposedly "professional" scientific journals giving "objective" scientific analyses. However, science is based upon data, i.e., provable facts and not opinion—but are these opinions reflective of science? Thus, what is certain is that to the authors of these articles, it is important *to them* that homosexuality not be considered disordered.

Another example is from the American Psychiatric Association (APA).[133] In an attempt to support the legalization of same-sex "marriage" in California, the APA writes:

> The brief cites the scientific evidence concerning sexual orientation and family on key points, including that homosexuality is a normal expression of human sexuality; sexual orientation is not the result of voluntary choice; lesbians and gay men have stable, committed relationships similar to heterosexual couples in key aspects; and many same-sex couples are raising children and there is no evidence that gay and lesbian parents are any less capable than heterosexual parents.[134]

Each claim of the above quotation is controversial, can be contradicted, and reflects a non-scientific judgment:

(1) Who or what sets the "controls" in the classification for "normal" sexual expression? For instance, the commonness of a behavior does not necessarily equate with "normality"—rather, it is a disorder when a male or female who is biologically so does not reflect this in orientation, gender identity and social role;

(2) Some people do claim to "choose" homosexuality.[135] Also, there is a growing number of people who describe themselves as ex-gay or formerly same-sex attracted;[136]

(3) There is abundant statistical evidence which counters that lesbians and gays have stable relationships (they are, in fact, notorious for open promiscuity);[137]

(4) Only a percentage[138] of same-sex couples are raising children and the jury is still out on the effects of same-sex households on children since most studies claim that the healthiest among us are those raised with a mother and a father.[139] It should be added, this is certainly the case from a moral standpoint.

Lastly, it is not the place for psychiatrists or psychologists to give a definition of marriage. Marriage is not their proper scientific domain, nor is it even a subsidiary domain of their fields. Simply because such people might be "experts" in one particular area does not make them the authority on all areas of life. So, their authority or justification for same-sex "marriage" is unsound even by their own scientific principles. Furthermore, often the psychiatric and psychological academic and clinical communities are greatly divided, even within their own organizations, structures, and methodologies.

The Male and Female Distinction As the Basis of Marriage

Science is here illumined by the light of Revelation: "Jesus answered, 'Have you not read that the one who made them at the beginning "made them male and female,"' and said, 'For this reason a man shall leave his father and mother and be joined to his wife.'"[140] As with the Sacred Scriptures, the historic or traditional definition of marriage is based on the distinction of male and female and the natural complementarity of the two sexes. It is the interaction between the biological law of nature and the natural moral law. There is a disorder when this fundamental biological distinction is not accompanied by what could be described as the apparent sexual orientation, gender identity and social gender role. The word *apparent* is used because both the logical and real consequence of being male or female is that one's sexual orientation, gender identity and social gender role reflect the essential real biological distinction.[141] When one's sexual orientation, gender identity or social gender role does not reflect the essential real biological distinction of male or female, then the logical and real consequence is that there is a disorder. The American Psychological Association explains these terms in this way:

> *Sexual orientation* is distinct from other components of sex and gender, including *biological sex* (the anatomical, physiological, and genetic characteristics associated with being male or female), *gender identity* (the psychological sense of being male or female), and *social gender role* (the cultural norms that define feminine and masculine behavior) [emphasis added].[142]

Although the above terminology and distinctions are accurate and thus permissible to employ here in this assessment, when the American Psychological Association continues with its analysis of sexual orientation, several problems arise. The article continues with the following:

> Sexual orientation is commonly discussed as if it were solely a characteristic of an individual, like biological sex, gender identity, or age. This perspective is incomplete because sexual orientation is defined in terms of relationships with others. People express their sexual orientation through behaviors with others, including

such simple actions as holding hands or kissing. Thus, sexual orientation is closely tied to the intimate personal relationships that meet deeply felt needs for love, attachment, and intimacy. In addition to sexual behaviors, these bonds include nonsexual physical affection between partners, shared goals and values, mutual support, and ongoing commitment. Therefore, sexual orientation is not merely a personal characteristic within an individual. Rather, one's sexual orientation defines the group of people in which one is likely to find the satisfying and fulfilling romantic relationships that are an essential component of personal identity for many people.[143]

As was stated at the beginning of this section and in contradistinction to the authors of this quoted paragraph, the biological sex is not "solely" a characteristic of the person—rather, it is the fundamental or main principle when speaking of human sexuality. The individual is either male or female, and human sexuality plays off that inescapable binary.[144]

Sexual orientation and gender identity do or do not properly reflect a person's sex as male or female. If they reflect a person's sex as either male or female, then they are *ordered*. If they do not reflect a person's sex as either male or female, then they are *disordered*. Sexual orientation and gender identity also can be so disordered that an individual as an adolescent or adult could be attracted to same-sex or other-sex children or to animals, for that matter. Such real examples by themselves preclude the possibility of basing marriage on sexual orientation or one's gender identity. In the above citation from the American Psychological Association, then, sexual orientation, although promoted as being overarching, is not more fundamental than the category of male and female. Furthermore, in reality, sexual orientation does not define, as the American Psychological Association claims, inasmuch as it labels an attraction toward a group of people with whom a particular person is likely to identify or associate. In addition, sexual orientation is a descriptive for the sexual attraction and individual experiences not only toward other people but in some cases other animals or even inanimate objects. Sexual orientation is open to a swath of disorders and behavioral complexes. It should be obvious, then, that marriage is not based upon sexual orientation. Rather, marriage is between one man and one woman reflecting the ordered distinction and complementarity of the two sexes.

A More Thorough Explanation of Order

The Church's understanding of order and disorder is philosophical and follows a natural teleology. That is to say, the aim or end (*telos*) of an act or being in itself is to be taken into primary consideration when a determination is to be established. Likewise, there is a philosophical principle which states that act flows from or follows upon being.[145] Consequently, both acts and beings have a *telos*. In this understanding, the natural *telos* of human genital sexual expression (the act) is fundamentally and most obviously the propagation of the species, meaning the generation of new human life. Nature, as insurance and as an incentive to procreate, has also established that pleasure accompany genital sexual expression. This is the way we humans are set up; it is a law of nature. When genital sexual expression is not ordered to its natural *telos*, then it is disordered. In a similar way, sexual orientation and psychological gender identity are based upon being either male or female. Biological maleness and femaleness are primary to sexual orientation and psychological gender identity, meaning that sexual orientation and gender identity are founded upon being either male or female. From maleness comes a male psychological gender identity and an orientation toward the natural sexual complement: the female. From femaleness comes a female psychological gender identity and an orientation toward the natural sexual complement: the male. In this teleological way of viewing human sexuality, it is a disorder when from maleness a non-male psychological gender identity manifests itself or an orientation toward the unnatural sexual non-complement: the male. Likewise, it is a disorder when from femaleness a non-female psychological gender identity manifests itself or an orientation toward the unnatural sexual non-complement: the female. The obviousness of this recognition is given by nature itself in the impossibility of reproduction by same-sex sexual relations. It is upon this basis and understanding that the *Catechism* teaches in terms of the natural moral law that homosexual acts are *intrinsically* disordered, and that marriage is established between a male and a female.

Moreover, in this regard, sexual pleasure is deemed disordered when it does not accompany the naturally ordered sexual act open to the gift of life but is following after the *telos* of always impotent mutual or self-gratification.[146] Sexual pleasure is not a *telos* in itself. The *telos* or purpose of sexual pleasure is to act as a stimulus and in an accompanying role to the procreative act. It is secondary and founded upon the sexual act. Marriage, then, is not based on sexual pleasure nor on the intimacy which might accompany the sexual pleasure of mutual masturbation (female on female), same-sex penetration (male on male) or anal sex within marriage, for that matter. Conclusively, then, the Church's teachings in upholding the historic or traditional definition of marriage are not made-up, arbitrary, capricious, or imposed like those of same-sex "marriage" advocates, but are natural, reflective, logical, and universal.

Other Considerations

The current drive for same-sex "marriage," then, is an agendized push for a redefinition of marriage which dissolves the natural male and female distinction and complementarity in opting for sexual orientation (or expression) and the psychological sense of male or female. Social gender roles, it seems, would fall on both sides but would mainly favor the distinction of male and female and not orientation. The Catholic Church, then, is not being discriminatory or homophobic or repressive or only reverting to religion, faith and biblical authority in this matter (although all of these support her teaching). Thus, her understanding of marriage is not denying anyone a civil or basic human right. The Church is merely affirming that marriage is founded upon the natural biological distinction between a male and a female, whose complementarity is obvious and whose anatomy (when united) lends itself to the possibility of procreation.[147]

Same-sex couples lack and always will lack that mutual biological complementarity and the possibility of procreation through the sexual act. In fact, same-sex sex is impotent if one thinks about it biologically: vagina or finger/tongue on vagina or penis on anal/oral cavity are forms of sexual expression but are inherently non-life creating (one can here include also the simulation of sex by instruments)—that is, there is no lasting gift and union of such sex as there is in the sex between a male and a female in the possibility of a child.[148] These are "facts of life" which we all know and recognize to be the case.

These considerations do not deny or discount, however,

the possibility that two people of the same sex can be deeply in love with each other or have committed relationships; on the other hand, the same could be said of other types of relationships. It should be pointed out that an older male and a younger male (of minor age) companion or an older female and a younger female (of minor age) could also be deeply in love with each other and have committed relationships (or grandparents with their grandchildren, parents with their children, siblings with other siblings, aunts and uncles with their nephews and nieces)—but it should be obvious that none of these relationships qualifies for marriage.

Further, the prevalence of the phenomenon of persons who describe themselves with same-sex attraction is not a justification for a novel and forced definition of marriage. Although it stands to reason that for a long time there have been persons attracted to the same sex throughout the various cultures and civilizations, the factors are too many to preclude that there has always been the current number of people who identify themselves as such.[149] Same-sex attraction is linked closely with other factors which have accelerated in recent years: the modern breakdown of the family and the instability caused by the divorce of one's mother and father, the lack of or the overbearing nature of a male or female presence, failure to integrate psycho-sexually during childhood or adolescence, emotional difficulties, acute hormonal imbalances, etc.[150] While there is no pretense here to exhaust the origins of same-sex attraction, it seems likely that given these mainly developmental and environmental factors, the notion of having been always attracted to the same-sex is highly speculative and would be more accurately viewed as an issue of personal psychological formation.[151] This is all the more true when the nearly omnipresent and invasive influence of sexual relativism in society is taken into consideration.

[86]

CHAPTER V

Same-Sex "Marriage" and Society

In the previous chapter, a fundamental analysis of human sexuality and Church doctrine was given. Therein was explained why the Church teaches what she teaches regarding the properly ordered and complementary nature of the two sexes. We can now explore what happens when those distinctions are disavowed. When one slides down the slippery slopes and logical consequences of careless thinking, the ramifications are seen to be destructive and violent toward anyone who would be in opposition. Thus, society or civilization in general and its future are shown to be at risk of inundation by what can only be likened to a tsunami.

The "Logic" of Lady Gaga

In 2011, in addition to making an income of $90 million, Lady Gaga was the number-one overall ranked celebrity by Forbes Magazine. She was also considered in the following categories: number 1 in web, 1 in social, 2 in press, 3 in TV/Radio, 8 in money, and 11 among powerful women.[152] Like her or not, she is an impressive and influential presence in society. Combine her with her "Little Monsters," as she affectionately calls her followers, and there is a force to be reckoned with when she assigns her name to an agenda.

An example of this influential backing is her hit song entitled "Born This Way." As catchy as the rhythm might be, unfortunately, the song has at least three errors. The first two deal with perfection and imperfection. Firstly, from a theological and moral perspective, the human person is not born perfect as she suggests, but is rather born with an inherent inclination to sin and to do evil (the Catholic Church refers to this as Original Sin and concupiscence) and, therefore, in need of redemption. Secondly, we humans commonly have a wide range of physical, chemical, emotional and psychological imperfections and deficiencies depending upon our parents and our own development, health issues at various levels of gravity and undesirable characteristics. The five senses of sight, sound, touch, smell and taste also vary in degree from human to human, along with the perceptive capabilities of temperature, pain, hunger, thirst, equilibrium, and motion.

The third problem and the one which concerns us here is that Lady Gaga cloaks together "gay, straight, or bi, lesbian, transgendered life" with national origins ("Lebanese or Orient"), skin color ("black, white, beige, chola"), being poor or rich ("broke or evergreen") and disabled ("whether life's disabilities left you outcast, bullied or teased").[153] While she is right in standing up for those who might be considered outcasts because of sexuality, nationality, economic status or disabilities, she is wrong to conflate and thus blur these fundamentally very different issues. Here, before getting to the problem of the logic of "born this way," it serves to point out that although ethnic descent is invariable, one's nationality can change throughout life. Economic status is relative and disabilities can come about either through genetics or later on through disease or accidents.

As has already been mentioned, there are discernible developmental psychological and environmental factors which contribute to human sexual attraction. Science, however, cannot pinpoint such definite factors in the moment of the creation of our genetic makeup, and so it is unscientific to claim that one has always been a part of or is born into the gay, bi, lesbian, or transgendered life, as the song claims. In fact, living the LGBT "lifestyle" is the result of a decision. On the other hand, it is scientifically evident that one is born with a specific skin color as being descendant from a race of people—all humans are actually not only "born this way" but are "made this way" and are racially equivalent with accompanying basic and civil non-discriminatory human rights. In this regard, one commentator writes:

> The homosexual rights movement itself speaks of following upon and learning from the earlier civil rights and feminist movements. For without them there would be no homosexual rights movement today. But one parallel to these two previous movements cannot be made; they were about equality, racial and gender, for two distinct classes of individuals. There is no "homosexual" as a distinct class of individuals. "Homosexuals" are a group of individuals who self-identify by the behaviors they commit. . . . Yet the homosexual rights movement is well on its way to changing our society in greater ways than perhaps the combination of these two previous movements together. Homosexuals have been very successful in shifting the discourse from "behavior" to "rights." The homosexual rights movement is attempting to bring about change in our culture and society that is unprecedented in all of history, particularly in redefining gender and marriage.[154]

It would therefore be naïve not to consider "Born This Way" as agendized and ideologically driven. In point of fact, the song has become a standard-bearer in activism among LGBT groups.

Another consideration: If "being born this way" is the criterion for the legitimization of sexual expression, then it could be argued that people like Jerry Sandusky, the former defensive coordinator for Penn State University's football team, are not doing anything wrong by fulfilling their attraction for young boys or girls. Sandusky, then, was merely "born this way," could not help himself, and should be lawfully respected and maybe even encouraged. According to the logic of Lady Gaga, if his relationship with these boys is mutual and consensual, then why is there such discrimination in society? He is merely assisting them explore and mature in their sexuality as he was expressing his own. They are not disordered, they are just "born this way," and who is to be their judge? (In this context, it is important to acknowledge that unfortunately there are a growing number of groups advocating pederasty as simply normal and even healthy for adolescents, especially as a form of "education" to be promoted.[155])

Furthermore, what about those who are sexually attracted to their siblings, their parents, grandparents, aunts or uncles? How about those who are attracted to animals or corpses? Why should they be discriminated against? It is obvious that the *born-this-way* and therefore the *give-me-equal-freedom-of-public-sexual-expression-before-the-law-for-I-am-perfect* "logic" is inconsistent and false. Indeed, this way of thinking has dangerous consequences.

Social Acceptance of Same-Sex "Marriage"

Another aspect to this societal tsunami is the lowering and thus the weakening of personal inhibitions toward promiscuity and other immoral practices. With the increase of non-married cohabitation, divorce, contraception and abortion, the understanding of marriage as an exclusive lifelong covenant between one man and one woman has declined and has thereby opened up the social acceptance of same-sex partnerships.

In modern society, cohabitation is often cited as a way to save on expenses and to get to know a partner before making a commitment for life. However, contrary to such pro-cohabitation opinions, statistical data constantly show that cohabitating couples have a higher rate of divorce than those who did not live together before marriage.[156]

Objectively speaking, cohabitation is fornication (sex outside of marriage) or adultery (sex outside of marriage while being married) and is known as "living in sin."[157] From a moral standpoint, the sin is so grave that it is classified as deadly or mortal (since there is grave matter, knowledge and volition).[158] The destygmatization and frequency of divorce (often decided for any reason) and civil remarriage have cheapened the value of marital commitment. Contraception and abortion have created a promiscuous mentality, the commonplace degradation of women into sex objects, and have separated sex and marriage from procreation and child-rearing.

Furthermore, this decoupling of marriage from the creation of children (as in contraception and abortion) leads to the promotion of same-sex "marriage."[159] Regarding this issue, drawing from the thought of philosopher Elizabeth Anscombe, Douglas Farrow makes the following salient point:

> Contraceptive intercourse eliminates in principle the bond between the unitive and the reproductive, and with it any solid reason for confining sexual intimacy to the marital act.
>
> Broadly put, to embrace contraception is also to embrace the utilitarianism that governs the Bentha-

mite approach to sex. That approach sets aside the question of the intrinsic nature of an act, and of its ordering by the human agent to its proper ends, in order to concentrate solely on its capacity to maximize pleasure or happiness. But in doing so, it makes it impossible to distinguish morally between contraceptive and non-contraceptive intercourse, or between intercourse and other kinds of sexual activity, including sodomy, in a way that can sustain marriage as an institution that supports the natural family and is therefore of permanent public interest.[160]

So, in society-at-large, marriage is left weakened by this contraceptive and abortive mentality of pleasure and utility, thereby paving the way for the public approbation of same-sex relationships and eventually all other imaginable "relationships."

It is a mistake, as well, to consider marriage as merely a legally-binding contract that recognizes for a few years that two people are living together with tax benefits, promoting the cohabitation, contraceptive, and divorce mentality. The institution of marriage is not fundamentally about legal rights and benefits—many of which are already in place due to the recognized status of other relationships. Regarding this social and economic legal status, the USCCB makes the following observation:

> Some benefits currently sought by persons in homosexual unions can already be obtained without regard to marital status. For example, individuals can agree to own property jointly with another, and they can generally designate anyone they choose to be a beneficiary of their will or to make health care decisions in case they become incompetent. [161]

Does this way of thinking, then, not reflect a reductionist societal view of marriage in general? Is it any wonder, consequently, that there is a call to legalize what would be known as same-sex "marriage"?

Same-Sex Adoption, and the Expunging of Faith

If procreation is removed from marriage—from sexuality—then it is little wonder that the desire for children is demanded by those who cannot have children naturally due to their choices and disordered behaviors. In this light, it suffices here to point out that the deceptive brilliance of the screenwriters of the Emmy-winning ABC sitcom *Modern Family* is subtly to create a new set of social mores and values while at the same time, in reality, de-establishing and undermining the very concept of family, marriage, sexual identity and παιδεία (*paideia*: the education of children). In this way, the agenda of same-sex proponents is nationally (and internationally) sent forth without question or restraint. That is to say, *Modern Family* promotes the message that in the "modern family" there is nothing left for people of conventional faith, except for their ultimate dismissal.[162]

As an example of that dismissal in the real world and not the scripted one of television, in several of the various states and in the nation's Capital (Washington, D.C.) where adoption by same-sex couples has become legal, Catholic adoption agencies have been mandated and coerced by law either to comply and allow same-sex adoption or to shut down.[163] Of course, the Catholic adoption agencies have acquiesced by either closing or morphing their identity into nonreligious-affiliated entities. The deceitful nature of the agenda pushing the legalization of same-sex "marriage" is here merely pursued to its logical conclusion:

Every aspect of faith and morality is at stake and will be capriciously dismissed and then legally expunged. Sadly, does this not reflect (with stark clarity) an abject failure, spiritual poverty, pusillanimity and a vacuum of authentic Christian witness in the United States? To allow something so monumental and detrimental to occur without raising a coordinated and sustained defensive strategy to stop such an offence to the free exercise of religion and conscience that we have as Church under the First Amendment, is beyond comprehension.

Sexual Education in Public Schools

It perhaps goes without saying that same-sex "marriage" and adoption by same-sex couples lead to, or even necessitate, the indoctrination of children in public schools into the same-sex agenda and, consequently, its safeguarding by its promoters.[164] As the following quotation shows, the legalization of same-sex "marriage" is far from being morally neutral and has exponential repercussions when it comes to children and education:

> In Massachusetts, which legalized homosexual "marriage," children in second grade are taught in public schools that same-sex "marriage" is the same as traditional marriage, that they can grow up to marry either a boy or a girl, that either option is the same. What's more, parents cannot opt their children out of such "instruction."[165]

Those who push sexual education in schools—which often means advocating promiscuity, pornography, contraception, abortion and same-sex "marriage"—end up inhibiting the voice of the moral conscience (and is that not ultimately their goal?).[166] In this context, it should be noted that most Catholic children, teachers, principals, social workers, among others are not in Catholic schools, but in public schools. Of course, left to itself, regime ideology will enforce as much as possible "diversity training" in "alternative family structures," not only in these schools but everywhere else as well.[167]

On the other hand, for Catholics, if there is to be a sexual education program in government schools, then it should be voluntary but nevertheless include the following considerations. The children's parents or caretakers are to be present with the freedom to ask questions during the program itself and to discuss it with their children. If the parents are unable to be present, then the presentation should be video recorded and made available to the parents. The program should be rooted in the understanding of love and sexuality which are chaste. It should also be geared to informing children and adolescents that potentially any sexual activity as minors can be classified as a crime and is legally punishable (given that consensual sex among pubescent youth might not be easy to determine). These children and adolescents should be informed that there are laws that protect them and that they should report to the proper authorities as immediately as possible any verbal or physical sexual aggression toward them (including any incident which might happen off campus or with adults for that matter). Schools should provide a telephone hotline and an internet site for reporting sexual abuse which include a checklist of procedures to be followed by the school staff, along with a transparent connection to the local police department. If there is to be a sex education program in government schools, sexual activity should never be encouraged among students under the guise of so-called "safe-sex," nor should students be given a "sex packet" (with condoms or contraceptives which are controversial in nature and which promote habits and addictions of sexual activity and promiscuity among youth). In addition, in public schools it should be illegal for counselors to advise abortions or to recommend or accompany a minor to an abortion clinic.

Two Examples of the Gay Agenda

The gale force of the agenda goes on as demonstrated by the following two examples:

(1) In March of 2011 the Lesbian, Gay, Bisexual, and Transgender Resource Center of Texas A&M University (a public school) organized its fourth annual "Fun Sex Seminar" with the title "Butt Play." The Director described the event in the following way: "It was the week before Spring Break; much like alcohol issues, we wanted to prepare students for whatever behaviors they may engage in." [168] The sexually graphic video presentation was specifically meant to lower inhibitions toward and to promote during Spring Break anal sex for both female and male students as an exploration of a type of sex act they might have previously been too put off by to attempt.

In this video presentation there is nothing wholesome. There is nothing positive or good for the individual or for the family or for society in general. There is nothing of value for any person, especially for one desiring to live a moral, virtuous and decent life. It is moral decadence at full throttle. Furthermore, "Butt Play" was produced in part by tax-payer dollars and student fees which go toward the more than $100,000 annual budget of the LGBT Resource Center of Texas A&M.[169]

With the commonness of events such as this one by the various LGBT organizations across the United States, it is difficult to believe that those groups might actually be concerned with promoting a credibly good cause such as anti-bullying campaigns or instructive information regarding AIDS. For this event to be promoted on any college campus is deplorable. What is more, to discover that tax-payers and non-LGBT students paid for it, is outrageous.

(2) Dan Savage is a well-known Seattle and syndicated advice columnist and "pundit" on sex and relationships. Recently, he has become more popular through a video program he initiated to assist young people contemplating suicide on account of problems supposedly stemming from their sexuality.[170] He is same-sex attracted and as of 2005 "married" (via Vancouver) his male partner. An interview in June of 2011 records:

> Savage believes monogamy is right for many couples. But he believes that our discourse about it, and about sexuality more generally, is dishonest. Some people need more than one partner, he writes, just as some people need flirting, others need to be whipped, others need lovers of both sexes. We can't help our urges, and we should not lie to our partners about them. In some marriages, talking honestly about our needs will forestall or obviate affairs; in other marriages, the conversation may lead to an affair, but with permission. In both cases, honesty is the best policy.
>
> "I acknowledge the advantages of monogamy," Savage told me, "when it comes to sexual safety, infections, emotional safety, paternity assurances. But people in monogamous relationships have to be willing to meet me a quarter of the way and acknowledge the drawbacks

of monogamy around boredom, despair, lack of variety, sexual death and being taken for granted."

In their own "marriage," Savage and Miller practice being what he calls "monogamish," allowing occasional infidelities [thus far 9 times], which they are honest about.[171]

For Savage to hold these positions on marriage and to be such an outspoken advocate for the legalization of same-sex "marriage" is to point to the obvious logical and sound conclusion: He has no idea what marriage is. Dan Savage is merely a type, for his numbers are legion, and what he is really advocating and lives is not marriage. In actuality, he could be said to be a proponent of the social acceptance of relational nihilism and a lifestyle of deception. Furthermore, if one is sexually confused (as Dan Savage obviously is) or is unable to control his "urges" (as Savage admittedly cannot), then from the Catholic worldview marriage is not for such a person and he should make the mature and healthy decision to abstain from marriage. Although such people should be respected and treated with dignity, they have no ground for advocating for the legalization of same-sex "marriage" or calling it "equality" to condone their immoral behavior and sexual disorientation and confusion.

This example brings to light the truth that the immensely successful and influential "Dan Savages" of this world are not only about making the LGBT lifestyle an accepted establishment in contemporary society, but they are also fundamentally about destroying the reality and even the concepts of monogamy, marriage between a male and a female, gender distinction, and morality in general.[172] Is this not a warning not to be duped and drawn in by their media intelligence which allows them to manipulate?

Dangerous Modification of Language,
  Definitions, and Concepts

The growing strength of this agendized wave is evidenced in this quotation from *Salon* Magazine. There is within the gay activist coercive redefinition-of-marriage agenda an opinion that even goes beyond the "born this way" form of argumentation:

> As popular as the theory of female "erotic plasticity" has become in the field of sex research, it is hardly without its critics; and many researchers are more inclined to highlight the sexual similarities between men and women. But beyond the ongoing scientific debate, there's a strong political argument to be made against taking an unwavering "born this way" stance. Marta Meana, a clinical psychologist at the University of Nevada Las Vegas who has researched sexual fluidity, believes "it is a devil's bargain to argue for acceptance on the basis of biology," she explains. "The 'I can't help it' argument retains the idea that something is amiss. The truly progressive stance is that all people should be treated with respect, dignity and equality regardless of the mechanisms that led them to prefer having consensual sex with one group over another, at any point in time." [173]

Clearly, this "truly progressive stance" would have any form of consensual sexual expression enshrined in law. The legal consequences of this way of thinking are expounded upon by Douglas Farrow: "[W]ithout any fixed position on what is given in human nature, any manipulation of it can be defended as legitimate. And that is exactly what they want to achieve with this legislation [i.e., the move to replace biological sex with the more "malleable concepts of sexual orientation and gender identity"]. Gender fluidity is what they are after—meaning no fixed borders for sexual identity and no fixed rules for sexual self-expression." [174]

Farrow further writes: "For these bills are Trojan horses, which on closer inspection are designed not to protect a threatened minority [within the context of his argument is meant the transsexual and the transgender] but to entrench in law the notion that gender is essentially a social construct, based not in the natural order but in more or less arbitrary acts of human self-interpretation." [175]

Another consequence of the redefinition of marriage is the latent acceptance of polygamy and other non-monogamous relationships. Princeton Professor Robert P. George argues:

> If marriage is redefined, its connection to organic bodily union—and thus to procreation—will be undermined. It will increasingly be understood as an emotional union for the sake of adult satisfaction that is served by mutually agreeable sexual play. But there is no reason that primarily emotional unions like friendships should be permanent, exclusive, limited to two, or legally regulated at all. Thus, there will remain no principled basis for upholding marital norms like monogamy.
>
> Candid and clear-thinking advocates of redefining marriage recognize that doing so entails abandoning norms such as monogamy. In a 2006 statement entitled "Beyond Same-Sex Marriage," over 300 lesbian, gay, and allied activists, educators, lawyers, and community organizers—including Gloria Steinem, Barbara Ehrenreich, and prominent Yale, Columbia and Georgetown

professors—call for legally recognizing multiple sex partner ("polyamorous") relationships. Their logic is unassailable once the historic definition of marriage is overthrown.[176]

These statements by George are a reasoned reflection on the LGBT agenda and are part of what is at stake in upholding the definition of marriage.

Finally, it is not to be denied that a proposed redefinition of marriage stems from an idea of the State as absolute—totally, as in totalitarian. If nature does not change, yet a government can redefine what is of the natural order, a problem of enormous proportions is created and the arbitrariness is evidenced in that "what the State has the power to define, it has the power to define again and again, and even to dispense with."[177]

Marriage is a pre-political institution, meaning that it is prior to government and has existed longer than any government currently in the world. When an administration, a government, a department of justice says, then, that it cannot or will not defend marriage as the exclusive union between one male and one female and in fact sets out to affirm the opposite, a totalitarian and arbitrary way of looking at the world is in blossom. Citizens of this type of government should beware.

Of course, the effects of this totalitarian regime extend beyond borders. Thus, as evidenced already with contraception and abortion ("preventive services"), the government of the United States (along with other nations) routinely withholds or threatens to withhold humanitarian aid to developing nations which refuse legal recognition of same-sex partnerships or "marriage."[178] In other words, this is yet another attempt to push the gay agenda beyond all borders with a "comply or else" authoritarian attitude.

Militant Gay Activism

The many well-organized pro-same-sex "marriage" activist groups are not playing games; rather, they are industrious and armed with a staggering amount of money, lobbying techniques, human resources and grass-roots movements aimed at to repealing DOMA and making sure that their pro-same-sex "marriage" candidates win elections. In the past several years, they have been highly successful as the militant activist "Human Rights Campaign" (HRC) boasts on its website:

DEFEAT OF THE FEDERAL MARRIAGE AMENDMENT: Twice—in 2004 and 2006—HRC led the successful fight against the Federal Marriage Amendment, which would have banned marriage equality. The massive field and lobbying effort in 2004, coupled with a $1 million TV, print and online advertising campaign, effectively communicated the message that the FMA was discriminatory and unnecessary, and would undermine the U.S. Constitution. HRC led the way again in 2006, in a campaign that culminated in the delivery of nearly 250,000 postcards to Capitol Hill offices just ahead of a second congressional defeat of the FMA.

MARRIAGE IN THE STATES: Momentum is building for marriage equality—and the Human Rights Campaign is at the forefront of these state battles. In 2006, when Massachusetts was the only state to recognize equal marriage rights, HRC and its allies helped beat back anti-marriage amendments in New Hampshire and Iowa—and continued on-the-ground efforts through November to help win fair-minded majorities in both states' legislatures. This helped lay the groundwork for marriage equality in these states in 2008 and

2009, respectively./ HRC led the effort to enact marriage equality in the District of Columbia. It committed two full-time staff members who, working with coalition members, identified hundreds of supporters to testify before the DC Council; co-hosted a rally on the eve of the Council's vote; and hosted three of the first weddings at HRC headquarters. Additionally, the Religion and Faith program helped organize and sustain DC Clergy United for Marriage Equality, one of the key players in the fight./ Most recently, in the fight for marriage equality in New York, HRC led the largest field campaign ever in support of state LGBT rights legislation. An unprecedented 30 full-time field organizers were employed by HRC across the state and they generated over 150,000 constituent contacts to targeted legislators. To reflect the deep and diverse support for marriage equality, HRC also created "New Yorkers for Marriage Equality," a video campaign that eventually featured more than 40 iconic New Yorkers.

ELECTION HEAVYWEIGHTS: The success of HRC's electoral efforts has earned widespread recognition. Its Political Action Committee is among the *National Journal's* top-rated progressive PACs, as more than 90 percent of its endorsees win their elections. This success dates back to its first major electoral effort in 1982, when HRCF donated $140,000 to 118 congressional candidates. Eighty-one percent of those candidates went on to win./ In 2008, for the most recent presidential election, HRC engaged in the largest electoral campaign in the history of the organization - called Year to Win, an aggressive $7 million election effort to mobilize and motivate millions of LGBT and allied voters—and helped to elect more than 200 pro-equality congressional candidates.[179]

The above quotations are examples of political warfare propaganda at its finest. As has been mentioned, the language of "equality" or "pro-equality" by these various LGBT organizations is false, misguided and misleading. In essence, such language is a clever marketing technique used to sell their agenda. It is necessary to state that these activists are motivated and politically savvy, and have a strong strategic plan: to involve as many diverse influential people in all sectors of society (including and especially religious entities) in their promotion of the gay agenda until finally all opposition collapses either by succumbing to manipulation or by being duped or just simply caving in to the relentless barrage of attacks.

As if this were not enough, it is important that Christians be aware of activist judges who promote same-sex "marriage" and the gay agenda. Professor Robert P. George reasons in the following manner:

Now the fight may head to the U.S. Supreme Court. Following California's Proposition 8, which restored the historic definition of marriage in that state as the union of husband and wife, a federal lawsuit has been filed to invalidate traditional marriage laws./ It would be disastrous for the justices to do so. They would repeat the error in *Roe v. Wade*: namely, trying to remove a morally charged policy issue from the forums of democratic deliberation and resolve it according to their personal lights./ Even many supporters of legal abortion now consider *Roe* a mistake. Lacking any basis in the text, logic or original understanding of the Constitution, the decision became a symbol of the judicial usurpation of authority vested in the people and their representatives. It sent the message that judges need not be impartial umpires ... but that

SAME-SEX "MARRIAGE" AND SOCIETY

judges can impose their policy preferences under the pretext of enforcing constitutional guarantees./ By short-circuiting the democratic process, *Roe* inflamed the culture war that has divided our nation and polarized our politics. Abortion, which the Court purported to settle in 1973, remains the most unsettled issue in American politics—and the most unsettling. Another *Roe* would deepen the culture war and prolong it indefinitely.[180]

Proposition 8 banning same-sex "marriage" was passed in 2008 by the voting populace in California. In 2010, Proposition 8 was overturned by an activist judge who allegedly wished to "marry" his same-sex partner and so with vested self-interest senselessly decreed it void rather than deliberating it rationally.[181] This judicial activism should not be tolerated as it undermines state laws.[182] Moreover, it does an exponential amount of damage to the legitimate separation of governmental powers and the system of checks and balances.

*Intolerance and Hate Aimed toward
Religious Belief and Conscience*

None of us should be fooled into thinking that we would be untouched by the legalization of same-sex "marriage" and its many consequences. The same-sex "marriage" agenda affects the most basic categories of everyday life as the following example illustrates. Victoria Childress, an owner of a small local bakery in Des Moines, Iowa, along with being accused of discrimination and being labeled a "bigot," was boycotted and received a plethora of hate letters and e-mails. Why? The story unfolds as she refused to make a cake for the "wedding" of a lesbian couple. She told them politely that she was a Christian and that her religious beliefs did not allow her to accommodate their request. KCCI Des Moines reports:

> "I didn't do the cake because of my convictions for their lifestyle. It is my right as a business owner. It is my right, and it's not to discriminate against them. It's not so much to do with them, it's to do with me and my walk with God and what I will answer (to) him for," Childress said.[183]

In retaliation for the business owner's refusal during their private meeting, the lesbian couple went public and released the following statement to the local news station:

> Awareness of equality was our only goal in bringing this to light, it is not about cake or someone's right to refuse service to a customer. We are grateful for the outpouring of support we have received and hope that by stepping forward we have prevented someone else from experiencing the same type of bigotry.[184]

Here it is important to take note of a further aspect of the story: the way it is reported by the local news. The first report begins by trivializing Mrs. Childress' beliefs: "A same-sex central Iowa couple is embroiled in a fight with a local baker with strong beliefs over a wedding cake."[185] That characterization is inaccurate for her beliefs are not about a wedding cake, but are about what is written in the Bible, her personal relationship with Jesus Christ, and the dictates of her well-formed conscience. The second report begins with these words: "A central Iowa same-sex couple's wedding planning came to a sudden halt"[186]—that description sets up victims of discrimination (the lesbian couple) and the perpetrator (the woman with religious beliefs). Not only did the reporters paint Mrs. Childress as a bigot and a homophobe, but they determinedly backed it up in their interviews with several other bakeries in the area that would have been compliant in fulfilling the couple's request. The media also consulted a local LGBT advocacy group to enlist a scathing critique of the baker.[187] So much for objectivity as the reports leave the reader no doubt about the agenda of the local news station in Des Moines.

The legalization of same-sex "marriage" is not, then, an issue that affects only two people, but is rather something which fundamentally alters the way of life of each of us and threatens to violate our religious principles and consciences through coercive legal means. As was noted in the chapter on freedom of religion, the list of the detrimental practical consequences is considerable and is constantly being augmented. The words of Jesus in the Gospel of Matthew give great comfort to us Christians and apply to Mrs. Childress:

> "Blessed are those who are persecuted for righteousness' sake, for theirs is the kingdom of Heaven. Blessed are you when people revile you and persecute you and utter all kinds of evil against you falsely on my account. Rejoice and be glad, for your reward is great in Heaven, for in the same way they persecuted the prophets who were before you."[188]

Victoria is an example of a Christian with a well-formed conscience, a conscience adhering to the truth regardless of the consequences. That Christians are living in states where same-sex "marriage" is the law is reminiscent, then, of the Babylonian Captivity when the People of God were forced by threat of punishment to adhere to the "laws of the Babylonians," which were at great odds with the laws of the One Creator God.[189]

Immediate Goals

In the future, if the militant activists succeed, the Catholic Church and others who oppose them will be compelled by law either to comply, be deaf and silent, or face legal fines, jail time and sanctions for "hate crimes" and "discrimination."[190] The influential force behind the legalization of same-sex "marriage," then, is not like drops of water falling on a rock until it cracks in half; rather, it is a tsunami with the intention and power to sweep away the very bedrock of civilization—and the first effects of the winds and waves are already being experienced. A tsunami causes total alteration and destruction. Trying to clean up after a tsunami is not easy work, and no one wants to suffer such consequences. For that reason, Christians need to react quickly and comprehensively.

First, it is our duty to proclaim the truth regarding marriage as an exclusive union between one man and one woman. Supporting our proclamation of the truth must be first and foremost prayer accompanied by fasting, humility, solidarity, and personal witness of life.

Second, it is necessary to vote for candidates who support the Defense of Marriage Act (DOMA), which upholds federal recognition of marriage between one man and one woman.

Third, as Catholics it is imperative that we unite with other religious communities (i.e., Protestant and Evangelical, along with Jewish and Muslim) and other people of good will—and that we work together to reaffirm each individual state constitution which already defines marriage according to its historic meaning. For those states which may not have such a definition in place, an amendment to the individual state constitution should be proposed and placed on the ballot for the next election.[191] For those states that have coerced a redefinition of marriage and that issue marriage licenses to same-sex couples, we should seek to put a proposition on those state ballots to ban same-sex "marriage" and to affirm *real* marriage.

Finally, given the nature of earlier discussed issues, it is essential that this united approach be rooted in the respect for the fundamental right to life, without which the institution of marriage itself makes no sense.

Concluding Remarks

To the angel of the church in Laodicea, write: "The Amen, the faithful and true witness, the source of God's creation, says this: 'I know your works; I know that you are neither cold nor hot. I wish you were either cold or hot. So, because you are lukewarm [κλιαρὸς], neither hot nor cold, I will spit [ἐμέσαι] you out of my mouth.' " [192]

This image in the Book of Revelation of a beverage being vomited (ἐμέσαι), because it is neither hot nor cold but merely lukewarm, is a metaphor used to describe an early Christian community with only a halfhearted adherence to the Faith.[193] This κλιαρὸς (lukewarm, tepid, indifferent, apathetic) community makes Christ nauseated. The source of the apathy of the Mediterranean Laodiceans was that they had grown worldly and smug. They were self-absorbed and padded by their materialism and prosperity so much so that they had become indifferent to authentic Christian witness. They had gone astray.

Some twenty centuries later, lukewarmness and apathy are widespread in contemporary Christianity, and this is arguably one of the principal reasons for the various cyclical failures at many levels of government. Society is amok because Christians have been indifferent to the importance of moral issues and to policies of a dangerous nature which have infiltrated our civil communities and politics. We, in the United States, have put forward men and women for public office, and we have elected and continue to elect those whose views, either directly or indirectly when followed to their logical consequences, are inimical to the teachings of Jesus Christ. Our apathy is vicious, even deadly, and has penetrated our moral, spiritual, intellectual, communal and political ways of being. Society in general has gone astray and, sadly, so have many of our own.

In the United States, to be free to adhere to and to practice one's religion is set forth and protected in the First Amendment of the Constitution. It is not the right or purpose of the government to establish a religion or to dictate to its citizens the practice of one specific religion or any religion at all. Freedom of "religion" does not mean merely a freedom of "worship" confined to a particular building on a particular day at a particular hour. As humans, we are not religious only in a particular setting or at a particular time, but rather in every place and at all times. Nor does freedom *of* religion signify freedom *from* religion. The separation of Church and State does not mean pitting government against religion and excluding it absolutely from the public square and discourse as certain atheist groups and politicians suggest. Above all, freedom of religion means that conscience is protected from intrusion and violation by the government. Thus, should a public policy or procedure go against one's religious tenets or practices, the individual has the right respectfully to decline to participate and, if need be, even resist.

As we have considered, abortion is the direct and willful destruction of an innocent human person. It deeply wounds the human family and proffers no solution to any problem a woman might face at the beginning of the third millennium. Allowing abortion to occur, perpetuates a lie regarding autonomy and irrevocably snuffs out the life of another human person. Such an action turns womanhood and motherhood upside down as it is unconscionable that a mother would deliberately order the death of her own child. Moreover, it removes the foundation upon which all other rights and freedoms are based. Once life is treated arbitrarily, so is the rest of life's dimensions.

Due to its fundamental and natural relation to procreation and education, the definition of marriage is not open to redefinition—marriage has already been defined. Marriage is between one man and one woman. What is open to discussion are the practical ways in which we can assist those who find themselves attracted to persons of the same sex. Thus, for those who are Catholic and attracted to the same-sex, it is important that they be aided in living out the vocation of every baptized person to be faithful to Jesus and His commandments regarding chaste sexuality and thereby grow in personal holiness of life.[194] At the same time, as has been demonstrated, given the hostile forces of those pushing same-sex "marriage" at every imaginable level of society, for the Church to use no approach or merely a "soft approach" in affirming historic or traditional marriage would be equivalent to using bayonets to fight against the latest military drones. It is obvious who would win that societal battle. It is also naïve and delusional to think that such powers and principalities are harmless and will stop before they completely destroy civilization (especially in the West) as we Christians know it through having built it.

The themes covered in this book, then, are of a serious and important nature. Reasoned argumentation both on a philosophical and theological level has been given in order to explain and justify the Church's position on these issues. In this regard, it has been shown to be inexcusable for a Catholic politician to "appeal to his conscience" to dissent when the Magisterium has spoken definitively on abortion and same-sex "marriage," among other gravely immoral issues. To be personally or privately opposed to, but publicly for, abortion and "marriage" between members of the same sex is unjustifiable for anyone who claims to be a follower of Christ.

It goes without saying, then, that as Christians, we cannot be mere spectators in the public square but rather must be active and vocal participants who make our voices heard and our actions felt. If we stand idly by on the sidelines and merely observe the current political situation and climate and carry on with an attitude of "business as usual," the Church, her institutions and her future will be washed away. Therefore, it is time for us to deviate from the materialist, secularist, nihilist and fatalist script which is being dictated to us by our contemporaries and for us to recall the original playbook and our *raison d'être*: " 'Go, and make disciples of all nations, baptizing them in the name of the Father, and of the Son, and of the Holy Spirit, teaching them to observe all that I have commanded you.' " [195]

If as Christians and as Americans, we allow our consciences and freedoms to be violated and trampled upon, the continuation of the murder of over one million innocent children annually through abortion, and same-sex "marriage" with all of its consequences to become a norm and a matter of law, it will be in part because we are lukewarm failures and inauthentic witnesses to Christ. What is more, we will be following (if we are not already) in the path of the Laodiceans of old. Today, one can visit Laodicea, but there are no more Christians. What one finds are ruins of a city built on a hill and an outlying nation whose Christian roots are hardly identifiable.[196] Laodicea is a reminder to us in America of the consequences of a lukewarm faith when set up against hostile tsunamic forces whose intent is to destroy by every means possible Christianity and the Church.

Notes

INTRODUCTION

1 See The Pew Forum, "Global Christianity: A Report on the Size and Distribution of the World's Christian Population" (19 December 2011). Available from http://www.pewforum.org/Christian/Global-Christianity-exec.aspx; Internet; accessed 3 February 2012.

2 See The Pew Forum, "Global Christianity: Spotlight on the United States" (19 December 2011). Available from http://www.pewforum.org/Christian/Global-Christianity-united-states.aspx; Internet; accessed 3 February 2012. Also, see The Pew Forum, "Key findings and Statistics on Religion in America" (2007). Available from http://religions.pewforum.org/reports#; Internet; accessed 3 February 2012.

3 See President Abraham Lincoln, "The Gettysburg Address," (November 19, 1863). Available from http://showcase.netins.net/web/creative/lincoln/speeches/gettysburg.htm; Internet; accessed 3 February 2012.

4 For the proper distinction between *transcendentalese* and *mundanese*, see Robert Sokolowski, *Introduction to Phenomenology* (New York: Cambridge University Press, 2000), 57–61.

5 *Forming Consciences for Faithful Citizenship* is available online at http://www.usccb.org/issues-and-action/faithful-citizenship/. For a brief review of the document, see Thomas Peters and Archbishop Charles Chaput (Interview, 2008). Available from http:catholicvideo.blogspot.com/2011/08/thomas-peters-american-papist.html; Internet; accessed 7 February 2012.

CHAPTER I: RELIGIOUS FREEDOM

6 See Open Doors, "World Watch List." Available at http://blog.opendoorsusa.org/world-watch-list. Also, see Aid to the Church in Need, "Persecuted and Forgotten? A Report on Christians Oppressed for their Faith" (2011 ed.). Available at http://www.aidtochurch.org/pdf/P&F_FINAL.pdf.

7 This is meant for laws governing society in America established by the Europeans. Of course, the infringement upon the freedoms of the native populations and Blacks (in the main formerly not considered citizens) is to be acknowledged.

8 For a recent commentary on religious freedom by the Bishops of the United States, see United States Conference of Catholic Bishops Ad

Hoc Committee For Religious Freedom, "Our First, Most Cherished Liberty: A Statement on Religious Liberty" (12 April 2012). Available from http://www.usccb.org/issues-and-action/religious-liberty/our-first-most-cherished-liberty.cfm; Internet; accessed 12 April 2012.

9 See The Freedom From Religion Foundation (http://ffrf.org).

10 Constitution of the United States, First Amendment (15 December 1791). Available from http://www.usconstitution.net/const.html#Am1; Internet; Accessed 11 January 2012.

11 Also, there was concomitantly a significant Spanish and French presence (which would have been predominantly Catholic) in areas not controlled by the British.

12 Augustine, *De Civitate Dei*, IV, 4.

13 See Mt 22:21.

14 See Vatican II, Pastoral Constitution on the Church in the Modern World [*Gaudium et Spes*], 36.

15 Pope Benedict XVI, Encyclical Letter *Deus Caritas Est* (25 December 2005). Available from http://www.vatican.va/holy_father/benedict_xvi/encyclicals/documents/hf_ben-xvi_enc_20051225_deus-caritas-est_en.html; Internet; accessed 8 February 2012: no. 28a.

16 The mark "/" in quoted texts signifies the end of a paragraph.

17 It should be noted as well that the United States (along with other nations such as Great Britain) have been denying aid to developing nations who will not adhere to the rhetoric of "reproductive services" and the gay rights agenda.

18 Although this case was resolved by a unanimous (9-0) decision to uphold the "ministerial exception," the mere fact that it was ever an "issue" is problematic. See Supreme Court of the United States, Syllabus "Hosanna-Tabor Evangelical Lutheran Church and School v. Equal Employment Opportunity Commission et al." (11 January 2012). Available from http://www.supremecourt.gov/opinions/11pdf/10-553.pdf; Internet; accessed 2 February 2012.

19 Timothy Cardinal Dolan, "Threats to Religious Freedom Harm More Than Religion" (20 October 2011). Available from http://cny.org; Internet; accessed 2 February 2012.

20 Timothy Cardinal Dolan, "Threats to Religious Freedom Harm More Than Religion" (20 October 2011). Available from http://cny.org; Internet; accessed 2 February 2012.

21 Obviously, there are certain times when the government *should* curtail freedom of religion if the common good truly is at stake. For instance, if a religion or religious leader requires human sacrifice or initiations which involve murder, then the government would have the duty to intervene.

22 See Phil Lawler, "A 'Conscience Clause' Is Not Enough" (2 Au-

gust 2011); Available from http://www.catholicculture.org/commentary/otn.cfm?id=825; Internet; accessed 11 January 2012.

23 John Paul II, "Address to the European Parliament at Strasbourg" (1988). Quoted in Avery Dulles, *Models of the Church* (New York: Doubleday, 1974; 2002), 231.

24 USCCB, "The HHS Mandate for Contraception/Sterilization Coverage: An Attack on Rights of Conscience" (20 January 2012). Available from http://www.usccb.org/issues-and-action/religious-liberty/conscience-protection/upload/preventiveqanda2012–2.pdf; Internet; accessed 9 February 2012. Also, it should be noted that on 1 March 2012, the "Blunt Amendment," which was very similar to the "Respect for Rights of Conscience Act" (HR 1179/S. 1467), was defeated in the Senate.

25 For the press release regarding the Government mandate, see U.S. Department of Health and Human Services, "A Statement by U.S. Department of Health and Human Services Secretary" (20 January 2012). Available from http://www.hhs.gov/news/press/2012pres/01/20120120a.html; Internet; accessed 8 February 2012.

26 See John Paul II, Encyclical Letter *Centesimus Annus* (1991). Available from http://www.vatican.va/holy_father/john_paul_ii/encyclicals/documents/hf_jp-ii_enc_01051991_centesimus-annus_en.html; Internet; accessed 13 February 2012, no. 46: "As history demonstrates, a democracy without values easily turns into open or thinly disguised totalitarianism."

27 See Americans United for Life Legal Team, "Planned Parenthood's 'Fact Check' Fails to Address Vast Majority of Claims in AUL Report" (12 July 2011). Available from http://www.aul.org/wp-content/uploads/2011/07/AUL-Rebuttal-to-PP–7–11–11.pdf.

28 Daniel Cardinal DiNardo, "Statement for Respect Life Month" (26 September 2011). Available from http://www.usccb.org/about/pro-life-activities/respect-life-program/2011/upload/dinardo-respect-life-statement–2011.pdf; Internet; accessed 21 January 2012.

29 See Gn 1:26–27.

30 Cf, *Catechism of the Catholic Church*, no. 2244: Every institution is inspired, at least implicitly, by a vision of man and his destiny, from which it derives the point of reference for its judgment, its hierarchy of values, its line of conduct. Most societies have formed their institutions in the recognition of a certain preeminence of man over things. Only the divinely revealed religion has clearly recognized man's origin and destiny in God, the Creator and Redeemer. The Church invites political authorities to measure their judgments and decisions against this inspired truth about God and man: Societies not recognizing this vision or rejecting it in the name of their independence from God are brought to seek their criteria and goal in themselves or to borrow them from some

ideology. Since they do not admit that one can defend an objective criterion of good and evil, they arrogate to themselves an explicit or implicit totalitarian power over man and his destiny, as history shows./ no. 2245: The Church, because of her commission and competence, is not to be confused in any way with the political community. She is both the sign and the safeguard of the transcendent character of the human person. "The Church respects and encourages the political freedom and responsibility of the citizen."/ no. 2246: It is a part of the Church's mission "to pass moral judgments even in matters related to politics, whenever the fundamental rights of man or the salvation of souls requires it". The means, the only means, she may use are those which are in accord with the Gospel and the welfare of all men according to the diversity of times and circumstances.

31 See Gn 1:28; Gn 9:1; Ex 23:25–26; Dt 7:13–14; 1 Sm 1–2:10; Is 54:1ff; 1 Tm 2:15, etc. Also, in these passages is evidenced the biblical view that sterilization and small families were considered curses or the loss of divine favor.

32 Paul VI, Encyclical Letter *Humanae Vitae* (1968), no. 17. Available from http://www.vatican.va/holy_father/paul_vi/encyclicals/documents/hf_p-vi_enc_25071968_humanae-vitae_en.html;   Internet; accessed 30 January 2012.

33 For the text of the compromise, see Office of the Press Secretary (the White House), "Remarks by the President on Preventive Care" (10 February 2012). Available at http://www.whitehouse.gov/the-press-office/2012/02/10/remarks-president-preventive-care; Internet; accessed 11 February 2012.

34 John Garvey, Mary A. Glendon, Robert P. George, et al., "Unacceptable Compromise" (10 February 2012). Available from http://ndcec.blogspot.com/; Internet; accessed 11 February 2012.

35 See Katie Thomas, "Self-Insured Complicate Health Deal" (15 February 2012) in *The New York Times*. Available from http://www.nytimes.com/2012/02/16/business/self-insured-complicate-health-deal.html; Internet; accessed 16 February 2012: "But the administration announced the compromise plan before it had figured out how to address one conspicuous point: Like most large employers, many religiously affiliated organizations choose to insure themselves rather than hire an outside company to assume the risk./ Now, the organizations are trying to determine how to reconcile their objections to offering birth control on religious grounds with their role as insurers—or whether there can be any reconciliation at all. And the administration still cannot put the thorny issue to rest." Also, "Nationwide, 60 percent of workers with health insurance were covered by a self-funded plan in 2011, according to the Kaiser Family Foundation's annual survey of employer

health benefits. Among large employers, the number is even higher. Eighty-two percent of covered workers at companies of more than 200 employees had self-funded plans./ Insurance industry experts and Catholic groups said they did not know how many religiously affiliated organizations self-insure, but they said the number was likely to mirror the national trend. Many of the organizations are large employers, including hospital systems and universities."

CHAPTER II: THE CONSCIENCE

36 See Second Vatican Council, Dogmatic Constitution on the Church *Lumen Gentium* (21 November 1964). Available from http:// www.vatican.va/archive/hist_councils/ii_vatican_council/documents/ vat-ii_const_19641121_lumen-gentium_en.html; Internet; accessed 27 February 2012. Number 25 states:

"Among the principal duties of bishops the preaching of the Gospel occupies an eminent place. For bishops are preachers of the faith, who lead new disciples to Christ, and they are authentic teachers, that is, teachers endowed with the authority of Christ, who preach to the people committed to them the faith they must believe and put into practice, and by the light of the Holy Spirit illustrate that faith. They bring forth from the treasury of Revelation new things and old, making it bear fruit and vigilantly warding off any errors that threaten their flock. Bishops, teaching in communion with the Roman Pontiff, are to be respected by all as witnesses to divine and Catholic truth. In matters of faith and morals, the bishops speak in the name of Christ and the faithful are to accept their teaching and adhere to it with a religious assent. This religious submission of mind and will must be shown in a special way to the authentic Magisterium of the Roman Pontiff, even when he is not speaking ex cathedra; that is, it must be shown in such a way that his supreme Magisterium is acknowledged with reverence, the judgments made by him are sincerely adhered to, according to his manifest mind and will. His mind and will in the matter may be known either from the character of the documents, from his frequent repetition of the same doctrine, or from his manner of speaking.

"Although the individual bishops do not enjoy the prerogative of infallibility, they nevertheless proclaim Christ's doctrine infallibly whenever, even though dispersed through the world, but still maintaining the bond of communion among themselves and with the successor of Peter, and authentically teaching matters of faith and morals, they are in agreement on one position as definitively to be held. This is even more clearly verified when, gathered together in an ecumenical council, they are teachers and judges of faith and morals for the universal Church, whose definitions must be adhered to with the submission of faith.

"And this infallibility with which the Divine Redeemer willed His Church to be endowed in defining doctrine of faith and morals, extends as far as the deposit of Revelation extends, which must be religiously guarded and faithfully expounded. And this is the infallibility which the Roman Pontiff, the head of the college of bishops, enjoys in virtue of his office, when, as the supreme shepherd and teacher of all the faithful, who confirms his brethren in their faith, by a definitive act he proclaims a doctrine of faith or morals. And therefore his definitions, of themselves, and not from the consent of the Church, are justly styled irreformable, since they are pronounced with the assistance of the Holy Spirit, promised to him in blessed Peter, and therefore they need no approval of others, nor do they allow an appeal to any other judgment. For then the Roman Pontiff is not pronouncing judgment as a private person, but as the supreme teacher of the universal Church, in whom the charism of infallibility of the Church itself is individually present, he is expounding or defending a doctrine of Catholic faith. The infallibility promised to the Church resides also in the body of Bishops, when that body exercises the supreme Magisterium with the successor of Peter. To these definitions the assent of the Church can never be wanting, on account of the activity of that same Holy Spirit, by which the whole flock of Christ is preserved and progresses in unity of faith.

"But when either the Roman Pontiff or the Body of Bishops together with him defines a judgment, they pronounce it in accordance with Revelation itself, which all are obliged to abide by and be in conformity with, that is, the Revelation which as written or orally handed down is transmitted in its entirety through the legitimate succession of bishops and especially in care of the Roman Pontiff himself, and which under the guiding light of the Spirit of truth is religiously preserved and faithfully expounded in the Church. The Roman Pontiff and the bishops, in view of their office and the importance of the matter, by fitting means diligently strive to inquire properly into that revelation and to give apt expression to its contents; but a new public revelation they do not accept as pertaining to the divine deposit of faith."

37 See Acts 2:42 (Greek text).

38 See Pius XII, Apostolic Constitution, *Munificentissimus Deus* (1 November 1950): *A.A.S.* 42 (1950), p. 756; see *Collected Writings of St. Cyprian*, Letter 66, 8: Hartel, III, B, p. 733: "The Church [is] people united with the priest and the pastor together with his flock."

39 See First Vatican Council, Dogmatic Constitution on the Catholic Faith, "On Faith," Ch.3: Denzinger 1792 (3011).

40 See Pius XII, Encyclical *Humani Generis* (12 August 1950): *A.A.S.* 42 (1950), 568–69: Denzinger 2314 (3886).

41 Second Vatican Council, *Dei Verbum* no. 10 (18 November 1965). Available from http://www.vatican.va/archive/hist_councils/ii_vatican_council/documents/vat-ii_const_19651118_dei-verbum_en.html; Internet; accessed 9 February.

42 On a more spiritual and theological level, the latter or second judgment of conscience foreshadows the particular and final judgment of God on the deeds and omissions of the individual: which open to eternal life or eternal condemnation.

43 *Catechism of the Catholic Church*, no. 1776. See Vatican II, Pastoral Constitution on the Church in the Modern World *Gaudium et Spes* (7 December 1965). Available from http://www.vatican.va/archive/hist_councils/ii_vatican_council/documents/vat-ii_cons_19651207_gaudium-et-spes_en.html; Internet; accessed 2 January 2012, nos. 16–17.

44 *Catechism of the Catholic Church*, no. 1781.

45 The logic of the Sacrament of Penance and the process of sin, repentance and forgiveness can be further expounded. In this Sacrament, the Catholic acknowledges in a public way that he has sinned, asks God for forgiveness, promises with God's help (grace) to sin no more, and makes through penance a reparation for having sinned in the first place. It should be noted that the public nature of Confession (as an expression of God's incarnational presence in the Priest-Confessor, meaning: the preferential human or mediated approach that God takes in saving us) is extremely important in growing away from vice and moving toward virtue, in establishing a well-formed conscience and in guarding against the deadly sin of pride. As humans, it humbles us to express our sins before another person who listens to us, gives us counsel and communicates the words of Absolution (only God forgives sins). It is easy for us spiritually or mentally to deceive ourselves or to downplay God's presence within us by directly asking Him for forgiveness repeatedly within ourselves [there is nothing wrong with that practice]. The other person, on the other hand, adds the dimensions of objectivity, clarity, the bridging of the alienation gap between us and God and the community caused by sin, and the fact that no one likes to confess publicly the same sin over and over again (especially if it is to the same Priest-Confessor)—all of which spur us on to conversion and a deeper repentance and the awareness of the possibility of the need for further moral and spiritual growth.

46 The distinction between the natural moral law and the law of nature is explained in Chapter III.

47 Congregation for the Doctrine of the Faith (CDF), Instruction On the Ecclesial Vocation of the Theologian *Donum Veritatis* (24 May 1990). Available from http://www.vatican.va/roman_curia/congre

gations/cfaith/documents/rc_con_cfaith_doc_19900524_
theologian-vocation_en.html; Internet; accessed 2 January 2012., no. 38.

48 *Catechism of the Catholic Church*, no. 1780.

49 See *Code of Canon Law* (1983), ns. 747–755.

50 Is 5:20 (RSV).

51 See *Catechism of the Catholic Church*, no. 1782: "Man has the right to act in conscience and in freedom so as personally to make moral decisions. 'He must not be forced to act contrary to his conscience. Nor must he be prevented from acting according to his conscience, especially in religious matters.'"

52 In this regard, relevant here is the following commentary [See United States Conference of Catholic Bishops Ad Hoc Committee For Religious Freedom, "Our First, Most Cherished Liberty: A Statement on Religious Liberty" (12 April 2012). Available from http://www.usccb.org/issues-and-action/religious-liberty/our-first-most-cherished-liberty.cfm; Internet; accessed 12 April 2012.]: "In his famous 'Letter from Birmingham Jail' in 1963, Rev. Martin Luther King Jr. boldly said, 'The goal of America is freedom.' As a Christian pastor, he argued that to call America to the full measure of that freedom was the specific contribution Christians are obliged to make. He rooted his legal and constitutional arguments about justice in the long Christian tradition: 'I would agree with Saint Augustine that "An unjust law is no law at all." Now what is the difference between the two? How does one determine when a law is just or unjust? A just law is a man-made code that squares with the moral law or the law of God. An unjust law is a code that is out of harmony with the moral law. To put it in the terms of Saint Thomas Aquinas, an unjust law is a human law that is not rooted in eternal law and natural law (Martin Luther King Jr., 'Letter from Birmingham Jail,' April 16, 1963)./ It is a sobering thing to contemplate our government enacting an unjust law. An unjust law cannot be obeyed. In the face of an unjust law, an accommodation is not to be sought, especially by resorting to equivocal words and deceptive practices. If we face today the prospect of unjust laws, then Catholics in America, in solidarity with our fellow citizens, must have the courage not to obey them. No American desires this. No Catholic welcomes it. But if it should fall upon us, we must discharge it as a duty of citizenship and an obligation of faith. / It is essential to understand the distinction between conscientious objection and an unjust law. Conscientious objection permits some relief to those who object to a just law for reasons of conscience— conscription being the most well-known example. An unjust law is 'no law at all.' It cannot be obeyed, and therefore one does not seek relief from it, but rather its repeal."

53 Mt 22:21.

54 Acts 5:29.

55 *Catechism of the Catholic Church*, no. 2242. See Pastoral Constitution on the Church in the Modern World *Gaudium et spes*, no. 74 § 5.

56 For a solid analysis of the conscience and John F. Kennedy, see Charles J. Chaput, *Render Unto Caesar: Serving the Nation by Living Our Catholic Beliefs in Political Life* (New York: Doubleday, 2008), 119–157.

57 John F. Kennedy, "Speech on Faith" (12 September 1960) in John F. Kennedy Presidential Library and Museum. Available from http://www.npr.org/templates/story/story.php?storyId=16920600; Internet; accessed 7 January 2012.

58 See John F. Kennedy, "Speech on Faith" (12 September 1960) in John F. Kennedy Presidential Library and Museum. Available from http://www.npr.org/templates/story/story.php?storyId=16920600; Internet; accessed 7 January 2012. Currently, the number of Catholics is estimated at over 70 million. See The Pew Forum on Religion & Public Life, "Religious Affiliation: Summary of Key Findings." Available at http://religions.pewforum.org/reports; Internet; accessed 2 February.

59 John F. Kennedy, "Speech on Faith" (12 September 1960) in John F. Kennedy Presidential Library and Museum. Available from http://www.npr.org/templates/story/story.php?storyId=16920600; Internet; accessed 7 January 2012.

60 Ibid.

61 Ibid.

62 See John Paul II, Encyclical *Evangelium vitae* (25 March 1995): Available from http://www.vatican.va/holy_father/john_paul_ii/encyclicals/documents/hf_jp-ii_enc_25031995_evangelium-vitae_en.html; Internet; accessed 11 February 2012, ns. 69–71: "[69] In any case, in the democratic culture of our time it is commonly held that the legal system of any society should limit itself to taking account of and accepting the convictions of the majority. It should therefore be based solely upon what the majority itself considers moral and actually practices. Furthermore, if it is believed that an objective truth shared by all is de facto unattainable, then respect for the freedom of the citizens who in a democratic system are considered the true rulers would require that on the legislative level the autonomy of individual consciences be acknowledged. Consequently, when establishing those norms which are absolutely necessary for social coexistence, the only determining factor should be the will of the majority, whatever this may be. Hence every politician, in his activity, should clearly separate the realm of private conscience from that of public conduct.

"As a result we have what appear to be two diametrically opposed tendencies. On the one hand, individuals claim for themselves in the moral sphere the most complete freedom of choice and demand that the

State should not adopt or impose any ethical position but limit itself to guaranteeing maximum space for the freedom of each individual, with the sole limitation of not infringing on the freedom and rights of any other citizen. On the other hand, it is held that, in the exercise of public and professional duties, respect for other people's freedom of choice requires that each one should set aside his own convictions in order to satisfy every demand of the citizens which is recognized and guaranteed by law; in carrying out one's duties the only moral criterion should be what is laid down by the law itself. Individual responsibility is thus turned over to the civil law, with a renouncing of personal conscience, at least in the public sphere.

"[70] At the basis of all these tendencies lies the ethical relativism which characterizes much of present-day culture. There are those who consider such relativism an essential condition of democracy, inasmuch as it alone is held to guarantee tolerance, mutual respect between people and acceptance of the decisions of the majority, whereas moral norms considered to be objective and binding are held to lead to authoritarianism and intolerance.

"But it is precisely the issue of respect for life which shows what misunderstandings and contradictions, accompanied by terrible practical consequences, are concealed in this position.

"It is true that history has known cases where crimes have been committed in the name of 'truth.' But equally grave crimes and radical denials of freedom have also been committed and are still being committed in the name of 'ethical relativism.' When a parliamentary or social majority decrees that it is legal, at least under certain conditions, to kill unborn human life, is it not really making a 'tyrannical' decision with regard to the weakest and most defenseless of human beings? Everyone's conscience rightly rejects those crimes against humanity of which our century has had such sad experience. But would these crimes cease to be crimes if, instead of being committed by unscrupulous tyrants, they were legitimated by popular consensus?

"Democracy cannot be idolized to the point of making it a substitute for morality or a panacea for immorality. Fundamentally, democracy is a 'system' and as such is a means and not an end. Its 'moral' value is not automatic, but depends on conformity to the moral law to which it, like every other form of human behavior, must be subject: in other words, its morality depends on the morality of the ends which it pursues and of the means which it employs. If today we see an almost universal consensus with regard to the value of democracy, this is to be considered a positive 'sign of the times,' as the Church's Magisterium has frequently noted. But the value of democracy stands or falls with the values which it embodies and promotes. Of course, values such as the dignity of every human person, respect for inviolable and inalienable human rights, and the adoption of the 'common good' as the end and criterion regulating political life are certainly fundamental and not to be ignored.

"The basis of these values cannot be provisional and changeable 'majority' opinions, but only the acknowledgment of an objective moral law which, as the 'natural law' written in the human heart, is the obligatory point of reference for civil law itself. If, as a result of a tragic obscuring of the collective conscience, an attitude of skepticism were to succeed in bringing into question even the fundamental principles of the moral law, the democratic system itself would be shaken in its foundations, and would be reduced to a mere mechanism for regulating different and opposing interests on a purely empirical basis.

"Some might think that even this function, in the absence of anything better, should be valued for the sake of peace in society. While one acknowledges some element of truth in this point of view, it is easy to see that without an objective moral grounding not even democracy is capable of ensuring a stable peace, especially since peace which is not built upon the values of the dignity of every individual and of solidarity between all people frequently proves to be illusory. Even in participatory systems of government, the regulation of interests often occurs to the advantage of the most powerful, since they are the ones most capable of maneuvering not only the levers of power but also of shaping the formation of consensus. In such a situation, democracy easily becomes an empty word.

"[71] It is therefore urgently necessary, for the future of society and the development of a sound democracy, to rediscover those essential and innate human and moral values which flow from the very truth of the human being and express and safeguard the dignity of the person: values which no individual, no majority and no State can ever create, modify or destroy, but must only acknowledge, respect and promote.

"Consequently there is a need to recover the basic elements of a vision of the relationship between civil law and moral law, which are put forward by the Church, but which are also part of the patrimony of the great juridical traditions of humanity.

"Certainly the purpose of civil law is different and more limited in scope than that of the moral law. But 'in no sphere of life can the civil law take the place of conscience or dictate norms concerning things which are outside its competence,' which is that of ensuring the common good of people through the recognition and defense of their fundamental rights, and the promotion of peace and of public morality. The real purpose of civil law is to guarantee an ordered social coexistence in true justice, so that all may 'lead a quiet and peaceable life, godly and respectful in every way' (1 Tim 2:2). Precisely for this reason, civil law must ensure that all members of society enjoy respect for certain fundamental rights which innately belong to the person, rights which every positive law must recognize and guarantee. First and fundamental among these is the inviolable right to life of every innocent human being. While public authority can sometimes choose not to put a stop to something which-were it prohibited- would cause more serious harm, it can never presume to legitimize as a right of individuals-even if they are the majority of the members of society-an offence against other persons caused by the disregard of so fundamental a right as the right to life. The legal tolera-tion of abortion or of euthanasia can in no way claim to be based on respect for the conscience of others, precisely because society has the right and the duty to protect itself against the abuses which can occur in the name of conscience and under the pretext of freedom.

"In the Encyclical *Pacem in Terris*, John XXIII pointed out that 'it is generally accepted today that the common good is best safeguarded when personal rights and duties are guaranteed. The chief concern of civil authorities must therefore be to ensure that these rights are recog-nized, respected, coordinated, defended and promoted, and that each individual is enabled to perform his duties more easily. For to safeguard the inviolable rights of the human person, and to facilitate the perfor-mance of his duties, is the principal duty of every public authority.' Thus any government which refused to recognize human rights or acted in violation of them, would not only fail in its duty; its decrees would be wholly lacking in binding force »."

63 Instrumental in the writing of the "Speech on Faith" were Ted Sorensen, a Unitarian Universalist, and the then-Catholic but subse-quently Episcopalian John Cogley (a former editor of *Commonweal*).

64 John F. Kennedy, "Speech on Faith" (12 September 1960) in John F. Kennedy Presidential Library and Museum. Available from http://www.npr.org/templates/story/story.php?storyId=16920600; Internet; accessed 7 January 2012.

65 John F. Kennedy, "Speech on Faith" (12 September 1960) in John F. Kennedy Presidential Library and Museum. Available from http://www.npr.org/templates/story/story.php?storyId=16920600; Internet; accessed 7 January 2012.

66 Sanger (1879–1966) was a famous American eugenicist and founder of Planned Parenthood.

CHAPTER III: ABORTION

67 Modified from Rev. Dr. Kieschnick, "Pam's Story," in *Perspectives*, Volume III Number 15 (15 December 2011).

68 See "Conception Pictures Slideshow: The Amazing Journey From Egg to Embryo." Reviewed by Kathy Empen, MD (2 September

2011); Available from http://www.medicinenet.com/conception_pictures_slideshow/article.htm; Internet; accessed 18 January 2012. Slide n.1: "Conception: From Egg to Embryo": "At the moment when a lone sperm penetrates a mature egg, conception or fertilization takes place."

69 See "Definition of Embryo" in MedicineNet.com. Available from http://www.medterms.com/script/main/art.asp?articlekey=3225;Internet; accessed 18 January 2012: "The organism in the early stages of growth and differentiation from fertilization to, in humans, the beginning of the third month of pregnancy. After that point in time, it is termed a fetus." Therefore, even by this definition, from fertilization (conception) there is an embryo.

70 "Stages of Pregnancy Pictures Slideshow: See the 1st, 2nd and 3rd Trimesters of Mom & Baby." Reviewed by William C. Shiel, Jr., MD, FACP, FACR (1 September 2011). Available from http://www.medicinenet.com/stages_of_pregnancy_pictures_slideshow/article.htm; Internet; accessed 18 January 2012.

71 For a Catholic analysis of human "person," see *Catechism of the Catholic Church*, nn. 355ff. See Congregation for the Doctrine of the Faith, Instruction *Dignitatis Personae* On Certain Bioethical Questions (8 September 2008). Available from http://www.vatican.va/roman_curia/congregations/cfaith/documents/rc_con_cfaith_doc_20081208_dignitas-personae_en.html. See Congregation for the Doctrine of the Faith, "Instruction on Respect for Human Life in its Origin and on the Dignity of Procreation: Replies to Certain Questions of the Day" *Donum Vitae* (22 February 1987). Available from http://www.vatican.va/roman_curia/congregations/cfaith/documents/rc_con_cfaith_doc_19870222_respect-for-human-life_en.html.

72 See *Catechism of the Catholic Church*, nn. 355ff. See Congregation for the Doctrine of the Faith, Instruction *Dignitatis Personae* [On Certain Bioethical Questions] (8 September 2008). Available from http://www.vatican.va/roman_curia/congregations/cfaith/documents/rc_con_cfaith_doc_20081208_dignitas-personae_en.html. See Congregation for the Doctrine of the Faith, "Instruction on Respect for Human Life in its Origin and on the Dignity of Procreation: Replies to Certain Questions of the Day" *Donum Vitae* (22 February 1987). Available from http://www.vatican.va/roman_curia/congregations/cfaith/documents/rc_con_cfaith_doc_19870222_respect-for-human-life_en.html.

73 Benedict XVI, "Address to German Parliament" (22 September 2011). Available from http://www.radiovaticana.org/en1/articolo.asp?c=522737; Internet; accessed 21 January 2012.

74 Phil Lawler, "The Personhood Initiative: Mississippi Voters Fail a Reality Check" (9 November 2011). Available from http://

www.catholicculture.org/commentary/otn.cfm?id=860; Internet; accessed 21 January 2012.

75 See *Catechism of the Catholic Church*, no. 1954.

76 Ibid., no. 1955.

77 Ibid., no. 2242. See Paul VI, Declaration on Religious Freedom *Dignitatis Humanae* (7 December 1965). Available from http://www.vatican.va/archive/hist_councils/ii_vatican_council/documents/vat-ii_decl_19651207_dignitatis-humanae_en.html. See Congregation for the Doctrine of the Faith, "Instruction on Respect for Human Life in Its Origin and on the Dignity of Procreation: Replies to Certain Questions of the Day" *Donum Vitae* (22 February 1987). Available from http://www.vatican.va/roman_curia/congregations/cfaith/documents/rc_con_cfaith_doc_19870222_respect-for-human-life_en.html.

78 See *Catechism of the Catholic Church*, nn. 355ff. See Congregation for the Doctrine of the Faith, "Instruction on Respect for Human Life in Its Origin and on the Dignity of Procreation: Replies to Certain Questions of the Day" *Donum Vitae* (22 February 1987). Available from http://www.vatican.va/roman_curia/congregations/cfaith/documents/rc_con_cfaith_doc_19870222_respect-for-human-life_en.html.

79 See Planned Parenthood Federation of America, "Annual Report 2009–2010." Available from http://issuu.com/actionfund/docs/ppfa_financials_2010_122711_web_vf?mode=window&viewMode=doublePage; Internet; accessed 4 January 2012.

80 As merely one example, visit Planned Parenthood at http://www.plannedparenthood.org/health-topics/.

81 Planned Parenthood, "In-Clinic Abortion Procedures." Available from http://www.plannedparenthood.org/health-topics/abortion/in-clinic-abortion-procedures–4359.asp; Internet; accessed 18 January 2012.

82 Ibid.

83 Guttmacher Institute, "Facts on Induced Abortion in the United States" (August 2011). Available from http://www.guttmacher.org/pubs/fb_induced_abortion.html; Internet; accessed 18 January 2012.

84 Guttmacher Institute, "Facts on Induced Abortion in the United States" (August 2011). Available from http://www.guttmacher.org/pubs/fb_induced_abortion.html; Internet; accessed 18 January 2012.

85 See J.T. Finn, "Birth Control Pills Cause Early Abortions" (23 April 2005). Available from http://www.prolife.com/BIRTHCNT.html; Internet; accessed 2 February 2012.

86 See Kaiser Foundation, "Follow the Pill: Understanding the U.S. Commercial Pharmaceutical Supply Chain" (March 2005). Available from http://www.kff.org/rxdrugs/upload/follow-the-pill-understanding-the-u-s-commercial-pharmaceutical-supply-chain-report.pdf;

Internet; accessed 2 February 2012, p. 7. Also, see URCH Publications, The Global Market for Hormonal Contraceptives and Infertility Drugs, 2011–2018: Future Therapies for Birth Control and Reproductive Health (May 2011; 2nd Edition). Available from http://www. urchpublishing.com/publications/market_trends/global_ market_hormonal_contraceptives_infertility_drugs_2011–2018.html; Internet; accessed 2 February 2012. See Guttmacher Institute, "Facts on Contraceptive Use in the United States" (June 2010). Available from http://www.guttmacher.org/pubs/fb_contr_use.html; Internet; accessed 2 February 2012. Note that the study begins with the question, "Who Needs Contraceptives?" Unfortunately, the researchers fail to make the basic distinction between a "need" and a "want," along with the ethical implications involved.

87 See Mary Calderone, "Illegal Abortion as a Public Health Problem" in *American Journal of Public Health* Vol. 50, n/ 7 [July 1960]), 949. Available at http://ajph.aphapublications.org/doi/pdf/10.2105/AJPH. 50.7.948; Internet; accessed 9 January 2012.

88 See J.C. Willke, MD, "Illegal Abortions" in *Why Can't We Love Them Both?* Available from http://www.abortionfacts.com/online_ books/love_them_both/why_cant_we_love_them_both_27.asp; Internet; accessed 18 January 2012: "By the year before the U.S. Supreme Court decision which allowed legal abortion on demand in all fifty states, the death rate for illegal abortions had fallen to: 39 (With 25 additional deaths that year due to legal abortions.) Now abortion was legal in 50 states. Now back alley abortions should have been eliminated with their alleged toll of maternal deaths./ In 1973 there should have been a really sharp drop in women dying. The chart, however, shows that there was no such drop. The line didn't even blip. The previous rate of decline actually slowed, to flatten out in the late 70s and 80s. According to the U.S. vital statistics, as anyone can see, legalization of abortion did not save almost any women's lives. /But we've been told the opposite. Correct, but let's recap: Pro-abortionists claim that in 1972, the year before the Supreme Court legalized abortion, there were 1,000,000 illegal abortions and 5,000 to 10,000 women died. Actually only 39 women died—less than one per state per year."

89 Kevin Hayes, "Dr. Kermit Gosnell, Philadelphia Abortion Doctor, Accused of Killing 7 Babies with Scissors," CBS News (19 January, 2011). Available from http://www.cbsnews.com/8301–504083_162–20028896–504083.html; Internet; accessed 13 November, 2011.

90 Irin Carmon, "Abortion Pioneer: Defend Rights or Lose Them" in *Salon* (2 January 2012). Available from http://www.salon.com/2012/01/02/abortion_pioneer_defend_rights_or_lose_them/singleton/; Internet; accessed 21 January 2012.

91 Irin Carmon, "Abortion Pioneer: Defend Rights or Lose Them" in *Salon* (2 January 2012). Available from http://www.salon.com/2012/01/02/abortion_pioneer_defend_rights_or_lose_them/singleton/; Internet; accessed 21 January 2012.

92 See Jane Dreaper, "Abortion 'Does Not Raise' Mental Health Risk," in BBC News (9 December 2011). Available at http://www.bbc.co.uk/news/health–16094906; Internet; accessed 21 January 2012. Notwithstanding that this study is seemingly pro-abortion in nature, its conclusions make it clear that there are not post-abortion psychological or mental improvements for women who abort. Also, as a counter to this study's claim of an abortion not raising mental health risk, see Priscilla K. Coleman, "Abortion and Mental Health: Quantitative Synthesis and Analysis of Research Published 1995–2009," in *The British Journal of Psychiatry* (September 2011), 199:180–186.

93 Jane Dreaper, "Abortion 'Does Not Raise' Mental Health Risk," in BBC News (9 December 2011). Available at http://www.bbc.co.uk/news/health–16094906; Internet; accessed 21 January 2012.

94 Research available at www.afterabortion.org. Also, see Americans United for Life Legal Team, "Planned Parenthood's 'Fact Check' Fails to Address Vast Majority of Claims in AUL Report (12 July 2011). Available from http://www.aul.org/wp-content/uploads/2011/07/AUL-Rebuttal-to-PP–7–11–11.pdf.

95 See Mary Calderone, "Illegal Abortion as a Public Health Problem" in *American Journal of Public Health* (Vol. 50, n/ 7 [July 1960]), 952. Available at http://ajph.aphapublications.org/doi/pdf/10.2105/AJPH.50.7.948; Internet; accessed 9 January 2012.

96 Research available at www.afterabortion.org. Also, see Americans United for Life Legal Team, "Planned Parenthood's 'Fact Check' Fails to Address Vast Majority of Claims in AUL Report (12 July 2011). Available from http://www.aul.org/wp-content/uploads/2011/07/AUL-Rebuttal-to-PP–7–11–11.pdf.

97 Available at http://hopeafterabortion.com/.

98 Available at http://www.rachelsvineyard.org/.

99 Office of the Press Secretary (The White House), "On the 39th Anniversary of Roe v. Wade" (22 January 2012). Available from http://www.whitehouse.gov/the-press-office/2012/01/22/statement-president-roe-v-wade-anniversary; accessed 23 January 2012.

100 Jn 10:10 (NRS).

101 See Jn 14:6 (NRS).

102 Norma McCorvey and Gary Thomas, "Roe v. McCorvey." Available from http://www.leaderu.com/norma/nmtestimony.html; Internet; accessed 21 January 2012.

103 Norma McCorvey and Gary Thomas, "Roe v. McCorvey."

Available from http://www.leaderu.com/norma/nmtestimony.html; Internet; accessed 21 January 2012.

104 It was originally known as the "National Association for the Repeal of the Abortion Laws."

105 See Bernard Nathanson, "Confession of an Ex-Abortionist." Available from http://www.aboutabortions.com/DrNathan.html; Internet; accessed 22 January 2012.

106 See ibid.

107 Iibid.

108 Jas 2:17 (NAB).

109 See Avery Cardinal Dulles, "Catholicism and Capital Punishment" (April 2001) in *First Things*. Available at http://www.first things.com/article/2008/08/catholicism-amp-capital-punishment–21; Internet; accessed 28 February 2012.

110 It is important to note that other "life issues" such as euthanasia and suicide are also distinct from capital punishment.

111 Avery Cardinal Dulles, "Catholicism and Capital Punishment" (April 2001) in *First Things*. Available at http://www.firstthings.com/article/2008/08/catholicism-amp-capital-punishment–21; Internet; accessed 28 February 2012.

112 See Avery Cardinal Dulles, ibid. He goes into detail regarding each one of them:

"*Rehabilitation.* Capital punishment does not reintegrate the criminal into society; rather, it cuts off any possible rehabilitation. The sentence of death, however, can and sometimes does move the condemned person to repentance and conversion. There is a large body of Christian literature on the value of prayers and pastoral ministry for convicts on death row or on the scaffold. In cases where the criminal seems incapable of being reintegrated into human society, the death penalty may be a way of achieving the criminal's reconciliation with God.

"*Defense against the criminal.* Capital punishment is obviously an effective way of preventing the wrongdoer from committing future crimes and protecting society from him. Whether execution is necessary is another question. One could no doubt imagine an extreme case in which the very fact that a criminal is alive constituted a threat that he might be released or escape and do further harm. But, as John Paul II remarks in *Evangelium Vitae*, modern improvements in the penal system have made it extremely rare for execution to be the only effective means of defending society against the criminal.

"*Deterrence.* Executions, especially where they are painful, humiliating, and public, may create a sense of horror that would prevent others from being tempted to commit similar crimes. But the Fathers of the Church censured spectacles of violence such as those conducted at the

Roman Colosseum. Vatican II's Pastoral Constitution on the Church in the Modern World explicitly disapproved of mutilation and torture as offensive to human dignity. In our day death is usually administered in private by relatively painless means, such as injections of drugs, and to that extent it may be less effective as a deterrent. Sociological evidence on the deterrent effect of the death penalty as currently practiced is ambiguous, conflicting, and far from probative.

"*Retribution*. In principle, guilt calls for punishment. The graver the offense, the more severe the punishment ought to be. In Holy Scripture, as we have seen, death is regarded as the appropriate punishment for serious transgressions. Thomas Aquinas held that sin calls for the deprivation of some good, such as, in serious cases, the good of temporal or even eternal life. By consenting to the punishment of death, the wrongdoer is placed in a position to expiate his evil deeds and escape punishment in the next life. After noting this, St. Thomas adds that even if the malefactor is not repentant, he is benefited by being prevented from committing more sins. Retribution by the State has its limits because the State, unlike God, enjoys neither omniscience nor omnipotence. According to Christian faith, God 'will render to every man according to his works' at the final judgment (Romans 2:6; see Matthew 16:27). Retribution by the State can only be a symbolic anticipation of God's perfect justice.

"For the symbolism to be authentic, the society must believe in the existence of a transcendent order of justice, which the State has an obligation to protect. This has been true in the past, but in our day the State is generally viewed simply as an instrument of the will of the governed. In this modern perspective, the death penalty expresses not the divine judgment on objective evil but rather the collective anger of the group. The retributive goal of punishment is misconstrued as a self-assertive act of vengeance.

"The death penalty, we may conclude, has different values in relation to each of the four ends of punishment. It does not rehabilitate the criminal but may be an occasion for bringing about salutary repentance. It is an effective but rarely, if ever, a necessary means of defending society against the criminal. Whether it serves to deter others from similar crimes is a disputed question, difficult to settle. Its retributive value is impaired by lack of clarity about the role of the State. In general, then, capital punishment has some limited value but its necessity is open to doubt."

113 *Catechism of the Catholic Church*, no. 2258. See Congregation for the Doctrine of the Faith, Instruction, *Donum vitae* (22 February 1987). Available from http://www.vatican.va/roman_curia/congregations/cfaith/documents/rc_con_cfaith_doc_19870222_respect-for-human-life_en.html; Internet; accessed 11 February 2012, no. 5.

114 *Catechism of the Catholic Church*, no. 2267. See John Paul II, *Evangelium vitae* (25 March 1995), Available from http://www.vatican.va/holy_father/john_paul_ii/encyclicals/documents/hf_jp-ii_enc_25031995_evangelium-vitae_en.html; Internet; accessed 11 February 2012, ns. 56 & 69. Also, see Gen 4:10.

115 See Death Penalty Information Center, "Facts About the Death Penalty" (27 January 2012). Available from http://www.deathpenaltyinfo.org/documents/FactSheet.pdf; Internet; accessed 7 February 2012.

116 See Guttmacher Institute, "Facts on Induced Abortion in the United States" (August 2011). Available from http://www.guttmacher.org/pubs/fb_induced_abortion.html; Internet; accessed 18 January 2012.

CHAPTER IV: MARRIAGE AND ITS IMPOSTERS

117 *Catechism of the Catholic Church*, no. 2357.

118 For a biblical commentary on Genesis 19, see Jude 1:7. Also, see Lv 18:22 (RSV): "You shall not lie with a male as with a woman; it is an abomination." Of course, Gn 1:26–28, in its positive declaration on the nature and purpose of male and female, excludes homosexuality.

119 The Revised Standard Version (RSV) has been used in these passages.

120 On the Church's tradition, see: Congregation for the Doctrine of the Faith (CDF), *Persona Humana* (29 December 1975). Available from http://www.vatican.va/roman_curia/congregations/cfaith/documents/rc_con_cfaith_doc_19751229_persona-humana_en.html; Internet; accessed on 2 February 2012. It would be wrong to infer from *Catechism* no. 2358 ("They do not choose their homosexual condition") that people are "born this way." It should be taken within the context of no. 2357: "Its psychological genesis remains largely unexplained."

121 This chapter will follow the example given at *Courage* and will not label those with same-sex attraction as "gay" or "lesbian." See *The Courage Apostolate*, "Why doesn't *Courage* use the terms "gay" and "lesbian"? Available from http://couragerc.net/FAQs.html; Internet; accessed 2 February 2012: "Courage discourages persons with same-sex attractions from labeling themselves "gay" and "lesbian" for the following reasons: (1) The secular world usually uses those terms to refer to someone who is either actively homosexual or intends to be. When a person decides to "come out" and say "I am gay" or "I am lesbian," the person usually means "this is who I am—I was born this way and I intend to live this way. I have a right to find a same-sex partner with whom to have a romantic sexual relationship." To "come out" as being "gay" or "lesbian" doesn't usually mean "I have homosexual attractions and I have a deep commitment to living a chaste life."

(2) By labeling someone, we discourage those who may wish to try and move beyond homosexual attractions. Some people, especially young people, are able to further their psychosexual development with spiritual and psychological aid. If we labeled them "gay" and "lesbian," they might think there's no possibility of moving beyond these attractions. (3) There is more to a person than one's sexual attractions. Even if one experienced same-sex attractions for most of one's life, he is first and foremost a child of God created in His image. To refer to that person as "gay" or "lesbian" is a reductionist way of speaking about someone. We are even trying now to avoid using the term homosexual as a noun, or as an adjective directly describing the person (i.e., homosexual person). Although it takes more words, we prefer to speak of "persons with same-sex attractions." Fr. Harvey has said that, if he could, he would rename his first book *The Homosexual Person* to something else like *The Person with Homosexual Attractions*. There are people within the Catholic Church who might argue that those who label themselves "gay" or "lesbian" aren't necessarily living unchastely. That's true, but the implications of the terms in today's society don't commonly connote chaste living. Furthermore, they are limiting their own possibilities of growth by such self-labeling, and reducing their whole identity by defining themselves according to their sexual attractions. At *Courage*, we choose not to label people according to an inclination which, although psychologically understandable, is still objectively disordered."

122 Mt 5:27–28; see Ex 20:14; Dt 5:18.

123 This list is given in the *Catechism of the Catholic Church* (nos. 2351–2356) under "Offenses Against Chastity."

124 *Catechism of the Catholic Church*, no. 2360.

125 *Catechism of the Catholic Church*, no. 2361. See John Paul II, Apostolic Exhortation *Familiaris Consortio* (22 November 1981), no. 11. Available from http://www.vatican.va/holy_father/john_paul_ii/apost_exhortations/documents/hf_jp-ii_exh_19811122_familiaris-consortio_en.html.

126 Second Vatican Council, Pastoral Constitution *Gaudium et Spes*, no. 49 § 2.

127 *Catechism of the Catholic Church*, no. 2362.

128 See *Catechism of the Catholic Church*, no. 2363. From a theological standpoint, see *Catechism* no. 2214: "The divine fatherhood is the source of human fatherhood; this is the foundation of the honor owed to parents. The respect of children, whether minors or adults, for their father and mother is nourished by the natural affection born of the bond uniting them. It is required by God's commandment." Furthermore, see Ex 20:12; Eph 3:14–15; Prov 1:8; Tob 4:3–4.

129 See Robert Levey, PhD, "Gender Identity Disorder (Transsexualism)" (15 January 2010) in *Medscape Reference*. Available from http://emedicine.medscape.com/article/293890-overview #aw2aab6b3; Internet; accessed 1 February 2012. See Charles Socarides, MD, "Sexual Politics And Scientific Logic: The Issue Of Homosexuality," in *The Journal of Psychohistory* 19:3 (Winter 1992): "By declaring a condition [homosexuality] a 'non-condition,' a group of practitioners had removed it from our list of serious psychosexual disorders. The action was all the more remarkable when one considers that it involved the out-of-hand and peremptory disregard and dismissal not only of hundreds of psychiatric and psychoanalytic research papers and reports, but also of a number of other serious studies by groups of psychiatrists, psychologists, and educators over the past seventy years. . . ."

130 These groups are further discredited when they make other judgments which go contrary to sound reason and common sense. For example, the APA is now moving to put "shyness" and "bereavement" on the list of "disorders" in the manual DSM–5. See News-Medical, "Internet Addiction, Shyness, Defiance and Grief on Bereavement could be Mental Disorders—Debate on Proposed DSM–5" (13 February 2012). Available from http://www.news-medical.net/news/20120213/ Internet-addiction-shyness-defiance-and-grief-on-bereavement-could-be-mental-disorders-e28093-Debate-on-proposed-DSM–5.aspx; Internet; accessed 15 February 2012. Also, see "Coalition For DSM–5 Reform" for an example of contrary opinions from other peer experts. Available at http://dsm5-reform.com/.

131 Patricia H Bazemore, MD, "Homosexuality: Introduction, Definitions, and Key Concepts" (4 August 2011) in *Medscape Reference*. Available from http://emedicine.medscape.com/article/293530-overview; Internet; accessed 1 February 2012.

132 For instance, see Joseph Nicolosi, Ph.D., "The 2009 APA Task Force Report—Science or Politics?" (10 January 2010). Available at http://narth.com/2011/01/dr-nicolosi-on-the-apa-task-force-report/; Internet; accessed 15 February 2012: "The American Psychological Association (APA) has released its 'Task Force Report on Appropriate Therapeutic Responses to Sexual Orientation' (August 2009), a report issued by five psychologists and one psychiatrist who are all on record as supporting gay causes. . . . Chair: Judith M. Glassgold, Psy.D. She sits on the board of the *Journal of Gay and Lesbian Psychotherapy* and is past president of APA's Gay and Lesbian Division 44. Jack Drescher, M.D., well-known as a gay-activist psychiatrist, serves on the *Journal of Gay and Lesbian Psychotherapy* and is one of the most vocal opponents of reparative therapy. A. Lee Beckstead, Ph.D., is a counseling psychologist who counsels LBGT-oriented clients from traditional religious

backgrounds. He is a staff associate at the University of Utah's Counseling Center and although he believes reorientation therapy can sometimes be helpful, he has expressed strong skepticism, and has urged the
Mormon Church to revise its policy on homosexuality and instead,
affirm church members who believe homosexuality reflects their true
identity. Beverly Greene, Ph.D., ABPP, was the founding co-editor of
the APA Division 44 (gay and lesbian division) series, *Psychological Perspectives on Lesbian, Gay, and Bisexual Issues*. Robin Lin Miller, Ph.D., is
a community psychologist and associate professor at Michigan State
University. From 1990–1995, she worked for the Gay Men's Health
Crisis in New York City and has written for gay publications. Roger L.
Worthington, Ph.D., is the interim Chief Diversity Officer at the University of Missouri-Columbia. In 2001 he was awarded the '2001 Cata-
lyst Award,' from the LGBT Resource Center , University of Missouri
, Columbia , for 'speaking up and out and often regarding LGBT
issues.' He co-authored 'Becoming an LGBT-Affirmative Career Advi-
sor: Guidelines for Faculty, Staff, and Administrators' for the National
Consortium of Directors of Lesbian Gay Bisexual and Transgender
Resources in Higher Education." Also, see Gerard van den Aardweg,
Ph.D, "Homosexuality And Biological Factors: Real Evidence —
None; Misleading Interpretations: Plenty" in NARTH Bulletin (Winter 2005). Available from http://narth.com/docs/aardweg.pdf; Internet;
accessed 12 February 2012. "Whence this 19th century step-motherly
treatment of psychology by our present-day professors Mégevant? It is
because with few exceptions they are gay persons wedded to the gay
ideology. They are the Weinbergs, LeVays, Hamers, Baileys,
Hershbergers etc., who openly admitted that biological roots of homosexuality favor social acceptance of the gay agenda (and right they are).
It is in their interest to be single-mindedly biology-biased. And since
the gay ideology has become the party line in the official establishment
of the human sciences, inclusive of most professional journals, all
findings 'support' homosexuality's biologic origin and mental normality
or at least 'suggest' it. Free research and free thinking is taboo as soon
as it seems to threaten the gay cause. The ideologically distorted science thus produced and sponsored profoundly misleads the public. On
a deeper level, it is often motivated not by thirst for the truth, but by
the wish to rationalize or justify the normality sought by so many
persons who are committed to a sexually abnormal lifestyle."

133 In my research, APA was found to denote also the American
Psychological Association (which is a different group). However, APA in
my text will always refer to the American Psychiatric Association.

134 American Psychiatric Association, News Release "APA Joins
Amicus Brief in Support of Same-Sex Marriage" (15 November 2010).

Available from http://www.psych.org/MainMenu/Newsroom/News Releases/2010-News-Releases/APA-Amicus-Brief—California-Same-Sex-Marriage–11–16–10.aspx; Internet; accessed 27 January 2012.

135 See Alex Wichel, "Life After 'Sex,'" *The New York Times* (19 January 2012). Available from http://www.nytimes.com/2012/01/22/magazine/cynthia-nixon-wit.html?_r=2&pagewanted=3; Internet; accessed 27 January 2012. The article reports on the famous actress Cynthia Nixon and her recent comments: « "I gave a speech recently, an empowerment speech to a gay audience, and it included the line 'I've been straight and I've been gay, and gay is better.' And they tried to get me to change it, because they said it implies that homosexuality can be a choice. And for me, it is a choice. I understand that for many people it's not, but for me it's a choice, and you don't get to define my gayness for me. A certain section of our community is very concerned that it not be seen as a choice, because if it's a choice, then we could opt out. I say it doesn't matter if we flew here or we swam here, it matters that we are here and we are one group and let us stop trying to make a litmus test for who is considered gay and who is not." Her face was red and her arms were waving. "As you can tell," she said, "I am very annoyed about this issue. Why can't it be a choice? Why is that any less legitimate? It seems we're just ceding this point to bigots who are demanding it, and I don't think that they should define the terms of the debate. I also feel like people think I was walking around in a cloud and didn't realize I was gay, which I find really offensive. I find it offensive to me, but I also find it offensive to all the men I've been out with." » Also, check out the following further commentary on Cynthia Nixon and her choice [see Tracy Clark-Flory, "When Gay is a Choice," in *Salon* (24 January 2012), Available at http://www.salon.com/2012/01/24/when_gay_is_a_choice/; Internet; accessed 27 January 2012].

136 See National Association for Research and Therapy of Homosexuality (NARTH), "Statement on Sexual Orientation Change" (27 January 2012). Available at narth.com. Also, see Larry Houston, "Discrimination For Being Ex-Gay." Available from http://banap.net/spip.php?rubrique29; Internet; accessed 3 February 2012.

137 See Timothy J. Daily, Ph.D., "Comparing the Lifestyles of Homosexual Couples to Married Couples" (Family Research Council). Available from http://www.frc.org/get.cfm?i=IS04C02#edn12; Internet; accessed 3 February 2012: "Research indicates that the average male homosexual has hundreds of sex partners in his lifetime: The Dutch study of partnered homosexuals, which was published in the journal AIDS, found that men with a steady partner had an average of eight sexual partners per year [Maria Xiridou, et al, 'The Contribution of Steady and Casual Partnerships to the Incidence of HIV Infection

among Homosexual Men in Amsterdam,' *AIDS* 17 (2003): 1031]. Bell and Weinberg, in their classic study of male and female homosexuality, found that 43 percent of white male homosexuals had sex with 500 or more partners, with 28 percent having one thousand or more sex partners [A. P. Bell and M. S. Weinberg, *Homosexualities: A Study of Diversity Among Men and Women* (New York: Simon and Schuster, 1978), 308, 309; See also A. P. Bell, M. S. Weinberg, and S. K. Hammersmith, *Sexual Preference* (Bloomington: Indiana University Press, 1981)]. In their study of the sexual profiles of 2,583 older homosexuals published in the *Journal of Sex Research*, Paul Van de Ven et al. found that 'the modal range for number of sexual partners ever (of homosexuals) was 101–500.' In addition, 10.2 percent to 15.7 percent had between 501 and 1,000 partners. A further 10.2 percent to 15.7 percent reported having had more than one thousand lifetime sexual partners [Paul Van de Ven et al., 'A Comparative Demographic and Sexual Profile of Older Homosexually Active Men,' *Journal of Sex Research* 34 (1997): 354]. A survey conducted by the homosexual magazine Genre found that 24 percent of the respondents said they had had more than one hundred sexual partners in their lifetime. The magazine noted that several respondents suggested including a category of those who had more than one thousand sexual partners ['Sex Survey Results,' *Genre* (October 1996), quoted in 'Survey Finds 40 percent of Gay Men Have Had More Than 40 Sex Partners,' *Lambda Report* (January 1998): 20]."

138 American Psychological Association, "Answers to Your Questions: For a Better Understanding of Sexual Orientation and Homosexuality," (2008). Available from http://www.apa.org/topics/sexuality/sorientation.pdf; Internet; accessed 26 January 2012: "In the 2000 U.S. Census, 33% of female same-sex couple households and 22% of male same-sex couple households reported at least one child under the age of 18 living in the home."

139 On the claims of same-sex households, see Larry Houston, "What About the Children? A Review of Homosexual Parenting Studies" (26 May 2007) in *Inventing the "Homosexual"* (website). Available from http://banap.net/spip.php?article82; Internet; accessed 3 February 2012.

140 Mt 19:4–5a (NRSV). See Gn 1:27–28a: "God created mankind in his image; in the image of God he created them; male and female he created them. God blessed them and God said to them: 'Be fertile and multiply; fill the earth and subdue it.'"

141 See Douglas Farrow, "Blurring Sexual Boundaries" in *First Things* (March 2011). Available from http://www.firstthings.com/article/2011/02/blurring-sexual-boundaries; accessed 25 January 2012.

142 American Psychological Association, "Answers to Your Ques-

tions: For a Better Understanding of Sexual Orientation and Homo-sexuality," (2008). Available from http://www.apa.org/topics/sexuality/sorientation.pdf; Internet; accessed 26 January 2012.

143 American Psychological Association, "Answers to Your Ques-tions: For a Better Understanding of Sexual Orientation and Homo-sexuality," (2008). Available from http://www.apa.org/topics/sexuality/sorientation.pdf; Internet; accessed 26 January 2012.

144 On the transgendered and the transsexual, see Richard P. Fitzgibbons, M.D., Philip M. Sutton, and Dale O'Leary, "The Psycho-pathology of 'Sex Reassignment' Surgery: Assessing Its Medical, Psy-chological, and Ethical Appropriateness," *The National Catholic Bioethics Quarterly* (Spring 2009), 97–125. Available from http://www.ncbcenter.org/Document.Doc?id=99; Internet; accessed 26 January 2012. See Robert Levey, PhD, "Gender Identity Disorder (Trans-sexualism)" (15 January 2010) in *Medscape Reference*. Available at http://emedicine.medscape.com/article/293890-overview#aw2aab6b3; Internet; accessed 26 January 2012. Also, for more infor-mation, see narth.com and see Paul McHugh, M.D., "Surgical Sex" (November 2004) in *First Things*. Available from http://www.firstthings.com/article/2009/02/surgical-sex—35; Internet; accessed 26 January 2012. In reality, the notion of having a "sex change" is really a misnomer and an impossibility. See National Catholic Bioethics Center, "FAQ on Gender Identity Disorder and 'Sex Change' Operations." Available from http://www.ncbcenter.org/page.aspx?pid=1039; Internet; accessed 26 January 2012: *What is a sex-change operation?* A typical sex-change operation is two-pronged. First, the person undergoes rather extensive psychological testing. Then he is placed on a hormonal regimen, and then, he undergoes surgery where the (original) genitalia are removed and replaced with the desired genitalia. In the case of a male-to-female surgery, for example, the penis is removed along with the testicles and in their place a make-shift vagina is constructed. For a female-to-male operation the woman undergoes a hysterectomy and mastectomy and a non-functional penis is constructed and attached. A sex-change operation invariably renders the person infertile. It should be noted that the hormonal regimen continues the rest of the person's life so that the secondary sexual characteristics can be maintained, e.g., a higher or lower voice, the presence or absence of facial hair, etc./ A sex-change operation should be distinguished from certain procedures per-formed on sexually ambiguous persons, for example, those suffering from congenital adrenal hyperplasia (a species of which is androgen insensitivity syndrome), mosaicism, chimerism, or some other congeni-tal cause of mixed sexual identity. These disorders present ambiguous sexual identity and certain operations done to confirm a person in the

'dominant' sex aims to correct a pathological condition. Such operations should not be thought of as changing a person's sex, but rather confirming what is originally ambiguous./ *What is immoral about a sex-change operation?* Properly understood, a person cannot change his sexual identity. For persons not suffering the disorders mentioned above (e.g., hermaphroditism) a person is either male or female. . . . We are either male or female persons, and nothing can change that. A person can mutilate his genitals, but cannot change his sex. Changing one's sex is fundamentally impossible; these procedures are fundamentally acts of mutilation./ Mutilation results in a person being rendered impotent or sterile and dependent for the rest of one's life on a hormonal regimen which makes one appear to be other than what he is. There is nothing wrong with the genitalia of persons seeking such operations. But they are removed in order to conform to the person's subjective belief about who he wants to be. Doing violence to one's body when there is nothing wrong with it is an unjustifiable mutilation. Furthermore, seeking such a mutilation manifests a self-hatred inconsistent with the charity we owe to ourselves. Persons seeking such operations are clearly uncomfortable with who they *really* are. Loving such persons properly demands addressing the beliefs and self-understanding that give rise to this fundamental rejection of self."

145 Known as *operari sequitur esse.*

146 This understanding is also involved in the Church's teaching on various forms of sexual genital expression (even masturbation) and contraception. The Church's teaching is clear because she is aware of human moral growth in freedom—the freest person is not the person driven by one's sexual passions (in fact, those persons are often the unhappiest), but rather the person with the greatest self-control and integration (known as the virtuous person whose passions and actions are integrated and properly ordered toward the human good). Each human person is called to chastity.

147 See Robert P. George, "Gay Marriage, Democracy, and the Courts: The Culture War Will Never End If Judges Invalidate the Choices of Voters," in *The Wall Street Journal* (13 August 2009). Available from http://online.wsj.com/article/SB10001424052970204619004574322084279548434.html; Internet; accessed 1 February 2012. Professor George examines this issue from a legal perspective. Marriage is properly viewed "as a union that takes its distinctive character from being founded, unlike other friendships, on bodily unity of the kind that sometimes generates new life. This unity is why marriage, in our legal tradition, is consummated only by acts that are generative in kind. Such acts unite husband and wife at the most fundamental level and thus legally consummate marriage whether or not they are generative in effect, and

even when conception is not sought./ Of course, marital intercourse often does produce babies, and marriage is the form of relationship that is uniquely apt for childrearing (which is why, unlike baptisms and bar mitzvahs, it is a matter of vital public concern). But as a comprehensive sharing of life—an emotional and biological union—marriage has value in itself and not merely as a means to procreation. This explains why our law has historically permitted annulment of marriage for non-consummation, but not for infertility; and why acts of sodomy, even between legally wed spouses, have never been recognized as consummating marriages./ Only this understanding makes sense of all the norms—annulability for non-consummation, the pledge of permanence, monogamy, sexual exclusivity—that shape marriage as we know it and that our law reflects. And only this view can explain why the state should regulate marriage (as opposed to ordinary friendships) at all—to make it more likely that, wherever possible, children are reared in the context of the bond between the parents whose sexual union gave them life."

148 It should be noted here that this argument is also at the root of the Church's ban on contraceptives and abortifacients, which detract from the natural complementarity reducing sex to pleasure or to a psychological release without the openness to new life as an expression of love between husband and wife. Also, it should be asked: What about the intergenerational aspects of the generative union which comes about through the conjugal act (the grandparents through their son or daughter onto the grandchildren)?

149 See See Larry Houston, "Types of Homosexualities" (26 May 2007) in *Inventing the "Homosexual"* (website). Available from http://banap.net/spip.php?article94; Internet; accessed 3 February 2012.

150 For a comprehensive approach to this subject, see National Association for Research and Therapy of Homosexuality (NARTH). Available at narth.com. Otherwise:

See American Psychological Association, "Answers to Your Questions: For a Better Understanding of Sexual Orientation and Homosexuality" (2008). Available from http://www.apa.org/topics/sexuality/sorientation.pdf; Internet; accessed 26 January 2012: "What causes a person to have a particular sexual orientation? There is no consensus among scientists about the exact reasons that an individual develops a heterosexual, bisexual, gay, or lesbian orientation. Although much research has examined the possible genetic, hormonal, developmental, social, and cultural influences on sexual orientation, no findings have emerged that permit scientists to conclude that sexual orientation is determined by any particular factor or factors. Many think that nature and nurture both play complex roles; most people experience little or no sense of choice about their sexual orientation." It should be noted that there is no mention of a so-called "gay gene" in that statement: see Dean Byrd, Ph.D., "American Psychological Association's New Pamphlet on Homosexuality De-emphasizes the Biological Argument" (6 March 2008). Available from http://www.narth.com/docs/deemphasizes.html.

See Stanton Jones, Ph.D, and Mark Yarhouse, Psy.D, Homosexuality: *The Use of Scientific Research in the Church's Moral Debate* (Downers Grove, IL: InterVarsity Press 2000): "Some researchers propose that human sexual orientation is determined before birth, probably between the second and fifth month of pregnancy. It is during this time that the fetus is exposed to sex hormones, its sexual anatomy develops, and its brain is 'wired' in a manner appropriate to its biological gender.... We should stress that hypothesized genetic and prenatal hormonal influences may be independent and exclusive of each other, or they may be interdependent and complementary. It is likely, indeed, that if there is a genetic element to the development of homosexuality, it probably works through prenatal and early childhood hormones."

Also, see Gerard van den Aardweg, Ph.D, "Homosexuality And Biological Factors: Real Evidence—None; Misleading Interpretations: Plenty" in NARTH Bulletin (Winter 2005). Available from http://narth.com/docs/aardweg.pdf; Internet; accessed 12 February 2012: "Whereas constitutional theories seem increasingly speculative, they are only the psychological correlates of homosexuality that are well-established. The highest correlations have systematically been found for what is currently designated as childhood and adolescent gender nonconformity: lack of integration in the boyhood/girlhood world and feelings of not belonging to the same-sex world. This syndrome has been established in clinical as well as nonclinical samples, in various countries and over several generations. Significantly, it is also recognized by authors who prefer to believe in biological theories (Hamer, LeVay, Bailey). The second-highest correlations exist with the finding of defective relations with the same-sex parent; the third-highest with maternal dominance/overprotection for the homosexual man, and with varied father factors for the lesbian. Empirically, then, a psychological explanation is the most realistic."

151 It is important to mention that the "nurture" argument (vs. "nature" argument) of same-sex attraction is gaining ground when the recognition of psychological development inside the womb (*in utero*) is considered. There are post-conception (meaning pre-natal) effects of the mother's psychological states on child development. See Association for Psychological Science, "Can Fetus Sense Mother's Psychological State? Study Suggests Yes" (10 November 2011) in ScienceDaily. com. Available from http://www.sciencedaily.com/releases/2011/11/111110142352.htm. Also, see The Association for Prenatal and Perina-

tal Psychology and Health (APPPAH) at http://birthpsychology.com/. Examples of relevant questions/implications would be: What are the pre-natal psychological effects of a mother (and father) on the child when a female was desired and prepared for instead of a male (or vice versa) by the mother (and father)? Or, in difficult relationships during pregnancy, when the mother felt (prolonged) animosity or hatred toward the father? Or, simply, when the father was not present during pregnancy? See Richard P. Fitzgibbons, M.D., Philip M. Sutton, and Dale O'Leary, "The Psychopathology of 'Sex Reassignment' Surgery: Assessing Its Medical, Psychological, and Ethical Appropriateness," *The National Catholic Bioethics Quarterly* (Spring 2009), 97–125. Available from http://www.ncbcenter.org/Document.Doc?id=99; Internet; accessed 26 January 2012.

CHAPTER V: HOMOSEXUAL "MARRIAGE" AND SOCIETY

152 *Forbes Magazine*, "Lady Gaga: Profile" (August 2011). Available from http://www.forbes.com/profile/lady-gaga/; Internet; accessed 10 February 2012.

153 See Stefani Joanne Angelina Germanotta (Lady Gaga), "Born this Way" (2011). Available from http://www.ladygaga.com/news/default.aspx?nid=33476; Internet; accessed 10 February 2012.

154 Larry Houston, "A Homosexual Agenda?" (26 May 2007) in *Inventing the "Homosexual"* (website). Available from http://banap.net/spip.php?article78; Internet; accessed 3 February 2012. He further expounds: "But when it is all said and done, as the homosexuals say and write in their books it is about societal approval for homosexual behavior. It is all about same-sex physical sex acts."

155 See North American Man/Boy Love Association (NAMBLA). Available at nambla.org. Also, another example in the general public is the Irish Senator (and a former 2011 Ireland presidential candidate) David Norris who advocates ephebophilia. See Helen Lucy Burke, "David Norris: The Free Radical" (January 2002) in *Magill Magazine*, 32–34. Available from https://sites.google.com/site/norrisarticle/; Internet; accessed 11 February 2012. Also, see Henry McDonald, "David Norris Still Sees His Destiny as Ireland's First Gay President" in *The Guardian* (12 June 2011). Available from http://www.guardian.co.uk/world/2011/jun/12/david-norris-ireland-gay-president; Internet; accessed 11 February 2012.

156 See Kathryn Jean Lopez, "No Way to Live: Cohabitation in America" (14 April 2008) in *National Review Online*. Available from http://www.nationalreview.com/articles/224058/no-way-live/interview; Internet; accessed 11 February 2012. In this interview, Michael McManus, the author of *Living Together: Myths, Risks & Answers, Couples,*

states the following: "Couples who live together are gambling and losing in 85 percent of the cases. Many believe the myth that they are in a 'trial marriage.' Actually it is more like a 'trial divorce,' in which more than eight out of ten couples will break up either before the wedding or afterwards in divorce. First, about 45 percent of those who begin cohabiting, do not marry. Those who undergo premarital divorce often discover it is as painful as the real thing. Another 5–10 percent continue living together and do not marry. These two trends are the major reason the marriage rate has plunged 50 percent since 1970. Couples who cohabit are likely to find that it is a paultry substitute for the real thing, marriage. Of the 45 percent or so who do marry after living together, they are 50 percent more likely to divorce than those who remained separate before the wedding. So instead of 22 of the 45 couples divorcing (the 50 percent divorce rate) about 33 will divorce. That leaves just 12 couples who have begun their relationship with cohabitation who end up with a marriage lasting 10 years." Also, see Center For Disease Control, "Cohabitation, Marriage, And Divorce" (2002). Available from http://www.psychpage.com/familymod_couples_thx/cdc.html#Z3 and http://www.cdc.gov/nchs/data/series/sr_23/sr23_022.pdf.

157 Here could also be mentioned the frequency and social acceptance of out-of-wedlock sex and childbearing.

158 See 1 Jn 5:16–17. Also, see *Catechism of the Catholic Church*, Available from http://www.vatican.va/archive/ccc_css/archive/catechism/p3s1c1a8.htm; Internet; accessed 3 February 2012, no. 1857 : "For a sin to be mortal, three conditions must together be met: 'Mortal sin is sin whose object is grave matter and which is also committed with full knowledge and deliberate consent.'"

159 Douglas Farrow, "Why Fight Same-Sex Marriage: Is There Really That Much at Stake?" (Jan.–Feb. 2012) in *Touchstone*. Available from http://www.touchstonemag.com/archives/article.php?id=25-01-024-f#ixzz1kOvgpMu7; Internet; accessed 24 January 2012: "The same-sex marriage issue and the abortion issue are joined hip and groin by contraception, and cannot be separated."

160 Douglas Farrow, "Why Fight Same-Sex Marriage: Is There Really That Much at Stake?" (Jan.–Feb. 2012) in *Touchstone*. Available from http://www.touchstonemag.com/archives/article.php?id=25-01-024-f#ixzz1kOvgpMu7; Internet; accessed 24 January 2012.

161 See USCCB, "Between Man and Woman: Questions and Answers about Marriage and Same-Sex Unions," no. 7 (www.usccb.org).

162 As merely one specific reference among the many possible, See Bron Taylor, "TV's Favorite Family Dumps Religion" (13 October 2010) in *rd Magazine*. Available from http://www.religiondispatches.org/

archive/culture/3538/tv%E2%80%99s_favorite_family_
dumps_religion/; Internet; accessed 5 February 2012.

163 See Human Rights Campaign, "Parenting Laws: Second Parent Adoption" (18 January 2011). Available from http://www.hrc.org/files/images/general/2nd_Parent_Adoption.pdf; Internet; accessed 5 February 2012.

164 See Shannan Martin, Robert Rector, and Melissa G. Pardue, "Comprehensive Sex Education vs. Authentic Abstinence: A Study of Competing Curricula" (2004); available at http://thf_media.s3.amazonaws.com/2004/pdf/67539_1.pdf; Internet; accessed 15 February 2012.

165 Stand For Marriage Maine (website). Available from http://www.standformarriagemaine.com/?page_id=115; Internet; accessed 15 February 2012. Also, in California, legislation and indoctrination as evidenced in "Senate Bill No. 48, Chapter 81. Available from http://info.sen.ca.gov/pub/11-12/bill/sen/sb_0001-0050/sb_48_bill_20110714_chaptered.pdf.

166 For an example, see Planned Parenthood, "Tools for Educators." Available from http://www.plannedparenthood.org/resources/. Also, see National Association for Research and Therapy of Homosexuality, "Gay Activism in the Schools." Available from http://narth.com/news-watch/gay-activism-in-the-schools/.

167 See Douglas Farrow, "Why Fight Same-Sex Marriage: Is There Really That Much at Stake?" (Jan.-Feb. 2012) in *Touchstone*. Available at http://www.touchstonemag.com/archives/article.php?id=25-01-024-f#ixzz1kOvgpMu7; Internet; accessed 24 January 2012.

168 GLBT Resource Center of Texas A&M, "Butt Play" (10 March 2011; video release 3 May 2011). Available from http://aggieconservatives.org/glbt; Internet; accessed 29 January 2012.

169 Ibid.

170 It should be noted that suicide is a complex and tragic phenomenon often stemming from multiple issues (not just one).

171 Mark Oppenheimer, "Married with Infidelities" in *The New York Times* (30 June 2011). Available from http://www.nytimes.com/2011/07/03/magazine/infidelity-will-keep-us-together.html?pagewanted=all; Internet; accessed 29 January 2012.

172 See Tracy Clark-Flory, "When Gay Is a Choice," in *Salon* (24 January 2012). Available from http://www.salon.com/2012/01/24/when_gay_is_a_choice/; Internet; accessed 27 January 2012].

173 See Tracy Clark-Flory, "When Gay Is a Choice," in *Salon* (24 January 2012). Available from http://www.salon.com/2012/01/24/when_gay_is_a_choice/; Internet; accessed 27 January 2012].

174 Douglas Farrow, "Blurring Sexual Boundaries" in *First Things* (March 2011). Available from http://www.firstthings.com/article/2011/

02/blurring-sexual-boundaries; accessed 25 January 2012. His initial quotation is from Doctor Paul McHugh of Johns Hopkins. Farrow is speaking in reference to bills proposed in Massachusetts and their counterparts in the different Provinces of Canada.

175 Douglas Farrow, "Blurring Sexual Boundaries" in *First Things* (March 2011). Available from http://www.firstthings.com/article/2011/ 02/blurring-sexual-boundaries; accessed 25 January 2012. The following is provided for a more thorough explanation:

"The definition of gender-related discrimination and of 'hate crimes' is becoming ever more imaginative on both sides of the forty-ninth parallel. Witness, for example, Bill H1728 in the State of Massachusetts, An Act Relative to Gender-Based Discrimination and Hate Crimes, or its Canadian counterpart, Bill C–389. The ostensible purpose of this legislation is to extend legal protection to 'sexual minorities.' The strategic intention, however, is something more ambitious.

"The American Civil Rights Act of 1964 prohibited discrimination based on 'race, color, religion, sex, or national origin.' 'Disability' and 'age' were soon added to this list, and later (by judicial interpolation) 'sexual orientation.'

"The aforementioned bills propose now to add to the list of protected categories 'gender identity and expression' or, more expansively, 'a gender-related identity, appearance, expression, or behavior of an individual.'/ . . . This has caused some consternation. Awkward questions are being asked about everything from cross-dressing males enjoying access to the ladies' room to insurance companies being forced to pay for sex reassignment therapy (SRT)—not to mention qualified surgeons being forced to perform it.

"First, observe that 'gender identity' and 'gender expression' are not, as proponents claim, like most other terms in these lists. That is, they do not represent objective conditions determined either by biology (like sex or race) or by sociopolitical institutions (like nationality, marital status, or religion). Rather, they represent subjectively determined conditions—mere attitudes toward oneself, or attitudes combined with behaviors (cross-dressing, say) intended to express or alleviate those attitudes. Gender identity, as one rights-commission statement puts it approvingly, 'is linked to an individual's intrinsic sense of self.

"The word 'sex' in our codes specifies the natural division of the species into male and female, with a view to protecting the latter especially. The addition of 'sexual orientation,' however, has effected a transformation in our thinking about human sexuality. Male and female have begun to give way to heterosexual and homosexual in the basic binary logic of sex. Hence the idea of same-sex marriage, with its air of legal inevitability.

"The proposed addition of 'gender identity and expression' carries that transformation even further by suppressing the binary logic itself. Backers of these bills often make no attempt to disguise this. 'One of the great myths of our culture,' insists the Canadian Labor Congress, 'is that at birth each infant can be identified as distinctly "male" or "female" (biological sex), will grow up to have correspondingly "masculine" or "feminine" behavior (public gender), live as a "man" or a "woman" (social gender role), and marry a woman or a man (heterosexual affective orientation). This is not so.

"The standard notion of sex, then, must be replaced by the more malleable concepts of sexual orientation and gender identity. And I do mean must. Here in Quebec a recent government white paper promises to wipe society clean of both homophobia and heterosexism—that is, of any 'affirmation of heterosexuality as a social norm or the highest form of sexual orientation [and of any] social practice that conceals the diversity of sexual orientations and identities.'

"Observe, as well, that these bills thinly veil another very telling contradiction. 'Trans' people, we are told—the people the bills are supposed to protect—are those who are uncomfortable with and to some extent reject the gender identities assigned to them at birth. Some are transsexual—namely, those who have a strong sense that they are living in the wrong sex'—and some are transgender, identifying with neither sex but placing themselves here or there on a gender spectrum. The former seek a transition between the two sexes; the latter deny that there are merely two sexes. The former may regard their problem as 'a medical concern, pure and simple,' to quote Corporal Natalie Murray of the Canadian Air Force, who made the transition. The latter often regard their problem as purely social, that is, as someone else's problem, the problem of bigotry.

"Here again we cannot easily have it both ways. Corporal Murray's 'hard-won identity as a woman' seems to make her a good poster girl for the Canadian bill, if one ignores the male chromosomes; but neither of these bills is about medical concerns, pure and simple. Medical concerns are covered by the term 'disability,' which is already in the list of prohibited grounds. In the final analysis, these bills are about the alleged bigotry. Which is to say, they are more interested in taking the transgressive out of 'transgender' than in guaranteeing the right to therapy for the transsexual."

176 Robert P. George, "Gay Marriage, Democracy, and the Courts: The Culture War Will Never End If Judges Invalidate the Choices of Voters," in *The Wall Street Journal* (13 August 2009). Available from http://online.wsj.com/article/SB10001424052970204619004574322084279548434.html; Internet; accessed 1 February 2012.

177 See Douglas Farrow, "The Audacity of the State: It's Bent on Bringing Down the House on the Family & the Church," in *Touchstone* (Jan.-Feb. 2010). Available from www.touchstonemag.com/archives/ article.php?id=23-01-028-f; Internet; accessed 24 January 2012.

178 Farouk Chotia, "Gay Rights: Africa the New Frontier" (7 December 2011), in BBC News. Available from http://www.bbc.co.uk/ news/world-africa–16068010; Internet; accessed 28 January 2012: "Mrs Clinton did not outline sanctions for countries that fail to reform same-sex laws, but an official memorandum directs US government agencies to consider gay rights when making aid and asylum decisions. Her comments follow a warning by UK Prime Minister David Cameron last month that the UK would reduce some aid to countries that refuse to recognize gay rights."

179 Human Rights Campaign, "Our Victories" (2011–2012). Available from http://www.hrc.org/the-hrc-story/our-victories; Internet; accessed 29 January 2012. Similarly, for example, see "Mission of the National Gay and Lesbian Task Force Foundation" Available from http://www.thetaskforce.org/about_us/mission_statements; Internet; accessed 29 January 2012: "The mission of the National Gay and Lesbian Task Force is to build the grassroots power of the lesbian, gay, bisexual and transgender (LGBT) community. We do this by training activists, equipping state and local organizations with the skills needed to organize broad-based campaigns to defeat anti-LGBT referenda and advance pro-LGBT legislation, and building the organizational capacity of our movement. Our Policy Institute, the movement's premier think tank, provides research and policy analysis to support the struggle for complete equality and to counter right-wing lies. As part of a broader social justice movement, we work to create a nation that respects the diversity of human expression and identity and creates opportunity for all./ The National Gay and Lesbian Task Force Action Fund, founded in 1974 as the National Gay and Lesbian Task Force, Inc., works to build the grassroots political power of the LGBT community to win complete equality. We do this through direct and grassroots lobbying to defeat anti-LGBT ballot initiatives and legislation and pass pro-LGBT legislation and other measures. We also analyze and report on the positions of candidates for public office on issues of importance to the LGBT community."

180 Robert P. George, "Gay Marriage, Democracy, and the Courts: The Culture War Will Never End If Judges Invalidate the Choices of Voters," in *The Wall Street Journal* (13 August 2009). Available from http://online.wsj.com/article/SB10001424052970204619004574 322084279548434.html; Internet; accessed 1 February 2012. Another article worth reading from Professor George is "What Happens When

Judges Decree Instead of Deliberate" (6 August 2010), in *The Washington Examiner*. Available at http://washingtonexaminer.com/node/470676; Internet; accessed 3 February 2012.

181 See Robert P. George, "What Happens When Judges Decree Instead of Deliberate" (6 August 2010), in *The Washington Examiner*. Available at http://washingtonexaminer.com/node/470676; Internet; accessed 3 February 2012. Also, for another example of activist judges, see Lisa Leff, "Prop 8, California's Same-Sex Marriage Ban, Declared Unconstitutional" in HuffPost (7 February 2012). Available from http://www.huffingtonpost.com/2012/02/07/proposition-8-california-same-sex-marriage-ban-ruling_n_1260171.html; Internet; accessed 9 February 2012: "Same-sex marriage moved one step closer to the Supreme Court on Tuesday when a federal appeals court ruled California's ban unconstitutional, saying it serves no purpose other than to 'lessen the status and human dignity' of gays."

182 One factor which is not treated thematically here is the burden same-sex legislation places upon the shoulders of the different states. It suffices merely to point out that such legislation creates a legal minefield.

183 KCCI Des Moines, "Wedding Cake Battle Brews Between Couple, Baker" [caption: "Couple: 'It Shouldn't Be Gay Or Straight Issue'"] (12 November 2011). Available from http://www.kcci.com/news/29753206/detail.html; Internet; accessed 9 January 2012.

184 KCCI Des Moines "Bakers Weigh in on Wedding Cake Controversy" (14 November 2011). Available from http://www.kcci.com/r/29763691/detail.html; Internet; accessed 9 January 2012.

185 KCCI Des Moines, "Wedding Cake Battle Brews Between Couple, Baker" [caption: "Couple: 'It Shouldn't Be Gay Or Straight Issue'"] (12 November 2011). Available from http://www.kcci.com/news/29753206/detail.html; Internet; accessed 9 January 2012.

186 KCCI Des Moines "Bakers Weigh in on Wedding Cake Controversy" (14 November 2011). Available from http://www.kcci.com/r/29763691/detail.html; Internet; accessed 9 January 2012.

187 Ibid.

188 Mt 5:11–12.

189 See Jer 39–43; 2 Kgs 25ff; 2 Chr; Dn 1–6; 1 Ezr 3:1–5:6.

190 In point of fact, as has already been pointed out, where same-sex "marriage" has been legalized Catholic adoption agencies have been forced to shut down or change their identity because they would not comply with the law in giving children over to same-sex couples for adoption. Also, in those States, our Catholic children (most of whom are in state-run or public schools) are being indoctrinated into the acceptance of same-sex "marriage" as a basic human right and the immoral

theory that any and all forms of consensual sexual expression are equally legitimate and to be explored.

191 See John Schwartz, "After New York, New Look at Defense of Marriage Act" (27 June 2011), in *The New York Times*. Available from http://www.nytimes.com/2011/06/28/us/politics/28doma.html?_r=1; Internet; accessed 3 February 2012: "Twenty-nine states have constitutional amendments that define marriage as being between a man and a woman, and 12 have laws that ban recognition of same-sex marriage."

CONCLUDING REMARKS

192 Rev 3:14–16 (NAB). For the Greek version, see *Strong's Concordance*. Available at http://biblos.com/revelation/3–16.htm.

193 I am grateful for the helpful commentary provided by the commentators on the New American Bible. Available at http://www.usccb.org/bible/revelation/revelation3.htm. A second interpretation of the reference to being "lukewarm" is that of the "hot springs of Hierapolis across the Lycus river from Laodicea, which would have been lukewarm by the time they reached Laodicea."

194 For example, see "The *Courage* Apostolate Homepage" at http://couragerc.net/. The *Courage* Apostolate Home Page reads: "*Courage*, an apostolate of the Catholic Church, ministers to persons with same-sex attraction and their loved ones. We have been endorsed by the Pontifical Council for the Family and our beloved John Paul II said of this ministry, '*Courage* is doing the work of God!' We also have an outreach called *EnCourage* which ministers to relatives, spouses, and friends of persons with same-sex attraction./ In Courage you will get to know men and women who share in your concerns, meeting them online through our Listservs, or in person at Chapter Meetings, Conferences, Days of Recollection, and Retreats. . . . From our website you will learn about same sex attraction and chastity. By developing an interior life of chastity, which is the universal call to all Christians, one can move beyond the confines of the homosexual identity to a more complete one in Christ." Also, see National Association for Research and Therapy of Homosexuality (NARTH) at http://narth.com/. The following is their Mission Statement: "We respect the right of all individuals to choose their own destiny. NARTH is a professional, scientific organization that offers hope to those who struggle with unwanted homosexuality. As an organization, we disseminate educational information, conduct and collect scientific research, promote effective therapeutic treatment, and provide referrals to those who seek our assistance. NARTH upholds the rights of individuals with unwanted homosexual attraction to receive effective psychological care and the right of professionals to offer that care. We

welcome the participation of all individuals who will join us in the pursuit of these goals."

195 Mt 28:19–20.

196 The ruins of ancient Laodicea are located in Turkey near the present-day town of Eski Hissar.

Made in the USA
San Bernardino, CA
03 December 2012